All About Winter Safety

Published by

World Publications

NORDIC BOOK SERIES NO. 5
March 1975

Library of Congress Catalog Card Number: 74-16794
ISBN: 0-89037-044-3

World Publications, Box 366, Mountain View, CA 94040

Contents

Illustrations by Bil Canfield.

Foreword

During the past decade the number of people who have taken to the winter outdoors on cross-country skis, snowshoes, snowmobiles, etc. has literally sky-rocketed. With that increase has come a need for more winter safety awareness and information. This book is an answer to that need.

All About Winter Safety does not attempt to cover all aspects of winter safety. The subject in its broadest sense would require several times the number of pages available here (and, in fact, there are books, such as *Medicine for Mountaineers* and *Mountaineering: The Freedom of the Hills,* both published by The Mountaineers, Seattle, Wash., which cover the subject in such detail). What this book does instead is offer practical safety information that every cross-country ski tourer and winter camper should know.

Generally people who go out on multi-day ski tours will have had some experience in summer backpacking and/or camping. They will, therefore, likely be competent in the skills necessary to survive in the summer environment. The winter environment, of course, is much more demanding. Thus the planning must be more precise. The equipment and clothing taken on a winter trip is more critical, and the technique more complicated (whether it's using map and compass to find your way in the snowy woods or being able to erect a tent in a howling snowstorm).

While accidents on ski tours and winter camping trips are relatively rare, when they do occur the consequences can be much more serious. Aid is usually more difficult to obtain, and the cold is a constant threat—particularly to someone who's injured and immobile. In winter, therefore, there's less room for accidents or errors of judgement, and a far greater demand for knowing *precisely* what to do in the event of error (such as getting lost), injury or some other unforeseen development.

To paraphrase a quote from our companion Nordic Series book *Snow Camping:* "Nature is beautiful in winter. But Mother Nature doesn't care about you. She is indifferent. Yet Mother Nature doesn't take lives. Man takes lives." There's a worthwhile lesson here for all winter recreationists. It says: While winter is indeed uncompromising, it's our own lack of planning, care and knowledge that really causes the tragedies, not some external force.

This book, although written with ski tourers and winter campers specifically in mind, is for all people who venture into the out-of-doors in winter. There's even a section on winter safety for the motorist. The book offers important information on technique and equipment, planning a trip, and using map and compass in winter. Separate articles are devoted to each of the major winter hazards—sudden weather changes, avalanches, frostbite, hypothermia, and dehydration. The longest chapter in the book, understandably, deals with medical aid, for both serious and minor injuries on the trail, and methods of evacuation.

Most of the people who have contributed to this book are professionals and experts in outdoor skills. They emphasize technical data, however, only to the extent that it makes for adequate understanding of the subject. Hence you are getting the best of both worlds—sound technical information, but only as it applies to basic winter safety.

This book deserves careful reading. The information on these pages could easily save a life—perhaps your own. After you have read the book, we would suggest you slip it into the side pocket of your pack near your first-aid equipment. It might be just the thing to read when the unexpected happens. Should you become injured, you can tell the other members of your group where the book is in your pack, and be assured that your companions will know how to take care of you.

We could not close without thanking publicly all the people who contribued to this book. Particular thanks must go to our friend and colleague Larry Moitozo, who played two major roles in the preparation of this book—chief contributor and technical editor.

1

Planning A Trip

Jim Rennie is the outdoor program coordinator at the University of Idaho in Moscow, Idaho, an experienced summer and winter outdoorsman, and a regular contributor to *Nordic World* magazine.

The route to the successful completion of a winter trip begins in the minds of the participants, rather than physically on the snow. A germ of an idea, liberally dosed with enthusiasm, provides the foundation of every trip. Unfortunately, many trips are long on enthusiasm and short on practical planning. Every trip has or should have a planning stage and the decisions made at this stage often prove more critical than the actual decisions made in the field.

Each field experience adds to the storehouse of information which will be used in planning succeeding trips. Not every outdoor experience is enjoyable, but even the "bombs" have some redeeming value in experience gained.

When planning a trip, the first step usually is to secure as much information as possible about the potential area. Geological Survey (topographic) maps will be very helpful. These can usually be found at public libraries but are also available at some stores, or you can get them through the mail from the US Geological Survey. (For areas west of the Mississippi River order from US Geological Survey, Federal Center, Denver, Colo. 80225; for areas east of the Mississippi, from US Geological Survey, Washington, D.C. 20242. Topographic maps of Canada may be purchased from the Map Distribution Office, Department of Mines and Technical Surveys, Ottawa, Ontario.)

These maps not only indicate the major landmarks of an area, but also show contour intervals. These contour lines indicate the steepness of the terrain. With this information, routes can be planned to avoid unnecesasry work and potential dangerous areas.

The only drawback to these maps is that they are sometimes out of date. (The date is listed in the lower margin of each map.) Roads and trails and other man-made features will often change with time. Maps which record these changes are available from the National Park Service and the Forest Service. These latter maps, which are used for fire prevention work, are kept up-to-date on access road and trail systems. They are usually available free from your local ranger district.

With map in hand it is often helpful to seek advice on your projected area from local outdoor clubs and individuals who may have previously taken a trip in that area. These groups in many cases have access to a great wealth of facts which may not otherwise be available. They may even put you in contact with other interested, and experienced, people for your trip.

When planning the route of travel on the map, you should take into account such potential problems as difficult terrain, avalanches, water sources and weather. While summer trails can be used as general guidelines for travel routes, it is important to realize that many summer routes are not easily followed in winter. Trail signs and blazes become obscured, and snow may make the terrain uneven and difficult to follow. The ski tourer has to contend with balance problems when carrying a pack. This is one good reason for selecting as easy a route as possible. Some trails follow the natural lines of weaknesses in the mountains, while others traverse steep mountainsides. These steep sidehill trails are more avalanche prone and more difficult to follow when snow covered. One advantage of the snow will be that some routes which are impossible to travel in the warmer months will become easier as the snow covers brush and downed logs.

The avalanche hazard is one dramatic problem to the winter traveller. Avalanches can occur without warning in a variety of conditions. Obviously, steep hillsides are always a potential threat. Cornices, or overhanging mounds of snow along the ridgetops may fall and trigger snowslides below. Changing temperatures may cause snow to slide, as will extremely heavy snowfalls in a short period of time. The best precaution is to become acquainted with what causes avalanches, where they occur and how to avoid them. Read the chapter later in this book on avalanche safety. There are also a number of excellent publications on avalanches published by the Forest and Park Services. In planning your tour, utilize the valley floors and the cover of trees as much as possible to minimize avalanche danger.

IMPORTANCE OF PROPER CLOTHING

During the planning process attention should be paid to proper clothing. Failure to take along the right clothing is perhaps the biggest contributing factor towards miserable outdoor experiences. Winter weather is variable and often devastating. Clothing must meet the demands of wind and water. But it must also provide proper ventilation. Even on a cold day it is important not to become too warm through exertion. This may lead to excessive perspiration which can rapidly chill a person when the exertion stops. This chilling may lead to hypothermia, which is a cooling of the body core (see "Hypothermia: The No. 1 Killer," page 50). Symptoms of this may be shivering or uncoordinated actions.

Perspiration and chilling can be prevented by taking a variety of clothing to adjust to the changing external temperatures and amount of exertion. Several light layers will be more suitable than only a couple of heavy ones. As the climactic conditions change, clothing can be added or taken off to ensure the proper heat ratio. Wool clothing will be by far the best value in outdoor garments. It will stay warm even when wet, something that cotton or down clothing cannot do.

You may need to take extra clothing to replace garments which become lost or get excessively wet. The best item of clothing for warmth will be a wool cap. The scalp is filled with blood vessels; as a result, you can lose a tremendous amount of heat through the head. Covering the head gives maximum warming to the entire body including hands and feet. When the body is overheated, the hat can be removed restoring normal temperatures to the torso and extremities. Clothing need not be fancy for outdoor wear, it only has to be functional. It should also be in good repair so that all zippers and closures work effectively and easily.

After considering clothing, a critical eye should be cast on various items of equipment which may be used for carrying the mountain of paraphernalia which we are often taking with us into the backcountry. Day trips are easy, requiring little more than a day pack to carry lunch, first-aid items, and extra clothing. The longer trips may require a pack frame similar to the ones used in the summer. On a higher scale are the assortment of rucksacks and softpacks that are specifically designed for travel in the snow environment.

The frame pack or rucksack is normally used to carry the entire trips' gear into a base camp. From there, a small day sack may be needed for daily sojourns on skis or snowshoes. Keep in mind that some things should always be close at hand. These include first-aid items, and extra clothing. The winter traveller should always have a small sack with him in which to carry such necessities.

A difficult problem for beginners will be achieving the right balance between enough gear and too much. Everything you take with you on a winter trip on skis must be carried and an overburdened person may have as many problems as the one who does not bring enough equipment to meet the needs of the trip. Basic necessities are important in winter. These have to do with needs of warmth, shelter, and personal care. Other items should be eliminated unless the person who carries them is aware of, and prepared to accept, their liability in terms of weight.

FOOD AND COOKING

Food is one of the most difficult and challenging preparation tasks. The demands of winter exercise require continued intake of calories, yet the demands of carrying many days' worth of food requires energy in itself. In planning the food to take the guidelines should be: 1) lightweight; 2) easy to prepare; and 3) palatable.

While there are many freeze-dried foods available today that are lightweight, the ordinary supermarket contains many foods that are just as suitable, and a lot less expensive. Meals can be devised best at home, and tested there before the trip. When you are cold and hungry on the trail, it's no time to discover that dinner is going to take 30 minutes longer to cook than you thought.

Foods and cooking should be kept simple. For instance, people have been eating oatmeal for years for breakfast. It's simple, hot and good for you. For the most part it only requires hot water; oatmeal, or the newer counterparts such as granola, will serve remarkably well for breakfast. Accompanied by hot chocolate and a biscuit, it should give you a good start to the day.

To save time on the trail, lunch is seldom cooked. An a la carte menu is ideal for the noon snack. Raisins, cheese, crackers, nuts and chocolate are the standbys of most outdoor parties. Again, such food is simple and very nourishing.

Dinner is usually the most elaborate meal of the day. Soups, stews and beef or chicken "glops" usually provide the foundation of a hot meal quickly followed by bed. There are plenty of varieties on this theme and experimentation is in order to find out individual preferences.

Buying all the food at the same time and repackaging it for maximum weight efficiency into daily rations or individual meals will help the sorting and organizing process greatly.

Most winter trips will require the use of a stove for cooking. Fire building in the snow is time consuming and difficult for cooking. Stoves will prove their superiority in a short time, although fire building materials should always be carried by each individual in any case.

Stoves do require practice in starting. The amount of fuel carried should be calculated on the daily amount to be used—the estimate should usually be on the high side. Too much fuel will mean extra weight, but too little is a far greater problem. Gasoline stoves have generally proven to be superior in winter use to pressurized butane or propane models which lose pressure in cold weather.

Larger groups or well organized parties may elect to use group cooking arrangements. The option on the other end of the spectrum is to eat individually prepared foods. It will require less organization for the group.

One other important point: make sure the stove works at home before using it in the field, and take plenty of matches.

SOURCE OF WATER

Winter activity requires as much or more intake of water as summer trips. Every effort needs to be made to find adequate sources of water. While melting snow is always a viable option, planning routes of travel to follow stream courses is far more prudent. Most individuals need three to four quarts of water per day in a winter environment, and melting snow is tiresome and fuel consuming. Streams are not always easy to get to when they're covered with ice and five to 10 feet of snow. But even the slower streams will have places where the water has not frozen.

Water can be obtained by lowering a pot on a string, or by stomping out steps down to the water source; lakes can be cut through if the ice is not too thick. Finding water will be a great aid to any trip, not only in offsetting dehydration and possible frostbite, but also in the pleasure of having a long cool drink when you need it.

Beginners to snow camping will probably get their introduction through several day trips before trying their hand at overnight excursions. These excursions are more difficult to plan than simple day trips, but more rewarding if planned right. Campsite and shelter selection will require experience to achieve the ultimate in comfort. In the meantime, it is important to buy or borrow a quality tent or shelter for use on the initial learning trips. If you don't sleep well, the whole trip may be ruined.

Tents need to be pitched in sheltered areas where the wind and the elements will not keep you up most of the night. Snow walls can be built as wind breaks in windy areas. Winter nights are long and the snow floor underneath the tent must be level in order for you to sleep comfortably. Summer backpackers who are now getting into winter camping should be aware that pitching the tent in the winter environment is different than in July. Just remember that the care you take in pitching the tent in the afternoon will be doubly rewarded by not having to get up in the middle of the night and redoing the job. Hopefully, the tent site will be near the water source.

FIRST-AID EQUIPMENT

One item that is often overlooked is the first-aid kit. Winter safety demands that each participant on an outing have his or her own kit to handle minor medical problems. A large group kit is needed for major problems. Commercially made kits are usually not very good. It is better to buy the items separately and make your own (see a list of items your first-aid kit should include on page 64). Outdoor stores such as Recreational Equipment in Seattle, Washington. (P.O. Box 22088, Seattle Wash. 98122), and Eastern Mountain Sports in Boston, Mass. (1041 Commonwealth Ave., Boston, Mass. 02215), have complete lists of first-aid items in their catalogues.

Particular attention should be paid to the repair of equipment. In the field regular wear and tear, the environmental conditions and carelessness will all begin to take their toll on equipment. It is most important to be able to repair equipment that breaks. It is either that or heading back home immediately. A repair kit should include tape, wire, needle and thread, pliers, screwdriver, safety pins, extra parts for equipment, and sundry other items. Each item of equipment should be evaluated and repair items carried for each.

In planning your trip, using the checklist method will be the most efficient and sure technique for not forgetting an item, and keeping things in order. Every item, no matter how small, should be listed and checked off as it is examined for condition and packed. Major groupings on the list will be food, cooking gear, shelter, clothing, first-aid, etc. A forgotten item may ruin your trip; careful checking will minimize this problem.

Rescue in the event of emergency is a final important consideration in planning any winter trip. While summer adventurers can usually count on mild conditions and speedy help much of the time, the winter skier-backpacker cannot, at least in many winter areas. In any case it is seldom possible to obtain rescue assistance in less than 24 hours after the rescue organization has been notified. This should encourage groups to make adequate preparations before they leave to ensure they can wait for a rescue, or accomplish their own.

On extended trips it is prudent to contact one of the local agencies and leave a plan of your trip. Should you fail to return, someone will know you are out there. Incidentally, many trips take longer than expected for a number of reasons. So set realistic times for returning. Your potential rescuers will appreciate it.

The planning of your winter trip will become easier the more often you go out, whether it be for a day or a week. There is no substitute for actual experience. And you'll find that the planning done before the trip will be invaluable when you actually get on snow.

Planning is the key to a safe winter trip. In the author's words: "The route to the successful completion of a winter trip begins in the minds of the participants, rather than physically on the snow. . . Every trip has or should have a planning stage, and the decisions made at this stage often prove more critical than the actual decisions made in the field." (Jack Miller photo).

Commonsense Safety Hints

by Virginia Meissner

Mrs. Virginia Meissner of Bend, Ore. probably has as much experience in the winter wilderness as any woman in North America. For 25 years she logged hundreds of miles per winter on cross-country skis as a snow surveyor (measuring the snowpack) in Oregon's Cascade Mountains. She now lectures on ski touring and winter camping at Central Oregon Community College, in Bend, Ore., and has her own cross-country ski school.

The following are bits and pieces of safety information I've gathered from experience. Some of the things I mention here are very simple—so simple, in fact, that they are often overlooked until it is too late. Simple or not, these hints are important and can mean the difference between a safe, enjoyable trip and a serious emergency.

Always take your survival kit. Even on a half-day trip you never know when there may be a need for the items in the kit.

Keep the group together. It is often the member of the group who becomes separated from the party who gets into difficulty. So whenever possible, keep the group together.

Observe the land around you. The ridges, valleys or mountains you see on the way out (look back as you go) may be the key to finding the way back.

Travel early in the day. In the springtime, travel is easier and safer early in the day when the snow is frozen. Spots where you might break through later in the day when the snow is soft may be solid enough when frozen so that they are safe to cross.

Don't depend upon following your tracks back. (1) The wind may cover then up with snow. (2) There may be a new snowfall before you return which will cover the tracks. (3) The sun may soften the snow so the tracks will no longer show. (4) Others may make tracks which cross or turn off from yours (so you'll be left wondering "Which tracks did I make?")

Pick a sheltered spot. When picking a place to camp, to stop for lunch or for an emergency, find a shelter that is: (1) out of the wind; (2) dry, or at least somewhat protected; and (3) free of obvious dangers such as avalanche, rising streams, etc.

Shelter may be found near trees or bushes, behind ridges or big rocks, or you can build a shelter by digging in the snow.

Look up! Look above you before camping under trees: (1) There may be dead limbs which will fall due to wind or weight of snow. (2) A pile of snow may fall off of the branches, hitting you or demolishing your tent. (3) Leaning snags may come down.

Try out your stove before you go.   Be very familiar with your stove and the rest of your equipment before you go. It's no fun to get out in the woods and find out you do not know how to make things work or that some small but important part is missing or broken. Keep the equipment in good repair.

Use extreme caution cooking inside a tent.   Almost every item in a tent is flammable, including the tent itself. Therefore, open flames of any kind should be avoided. If you *must* cook inside a tent, use extreme caution. Support the pot carefully when stirring, prime the stove with caution, do not overfill the stove with white gasoline so that the pressure valve is covered (if the excess valve allows pressure to escape, the excess gasoline will also shoot out). Be careful in refueling a stove. Make certain you don't spill any fuel and that the stove is cool. A hot stove can cause spilled fuel to explode. Make sure there is sufficient ventilation in the tent so there is no danger of carbon monoxide poisoning.

Smoke will attract attention. If you should become lost or if you need to stop where you are due to injury, illness or broken equipment, attention can be attracted by smoke from a fire. Smoke can be seen for a long distance, both from air and ground.

Use the water supply (e.g. a stream) to drink from but don't: (1) wash in it; (2) wash dishes directly in it; or (3) dispose of waste water too close to it.

Keep sanitary facilities back away from the water source. Pick a spot far enough away to be out of sight and out of the path of travel, and in an area where there is no drainage into the source of water.

Loss of equipment. If stopping on a slope, be careful that skis, poles or pack do not slide off down the mountain where they may become irretrievable.

Don't abandon broken equipment. It is easier to try to ski out on a broken ski than to try to walk when you will sink in deeply in the snow with every step.

Carry a butane cigarette lighter. A butane lighter maintains a steady flame and is, therefore, very useful for fire starting. The lighter can be warmed in the armpit should the butane freeze.

To start a fire, use small dry twigs, supported off the snow by a heavy log, thick bark, etc.

Ski wax will burn. Use this as a fire starter if you have no other.

Mittens are warmer than gloves because the fingers help to keep each other warm.

Springtime holes around rocks. When snow is melting, there may be big holes underneath the snow in and around big rocks. When taking off your skis near the rocks, ski right up to where you can step from the skis onto the rocks, thus avoiding breaking through the snow into a hole and possibly being injured.

Check snow bridges before crossing. If there is *any doubt* about a snow bridge, take another route or cross one person at a time on a belay. One way to check a snow bridge is by probing with a ski pole first.

Use your watch to improvise a compass. With the hour hand pointed at the sun, south is half way between the hour hand and twelve.

Take care when taking short cuts. Short cuts may be quicker, but often they will not be the safest route.

Use the moon to help find direction. The moon rises in the east and travels west just as the sun does.

Don't leave equipment in the snow. (1) It may get lost in the powder. (2) It may get snow kicked over it. (3) There may be a snowfall which will quickly cover the equipment.

Know when to turn back. Remember that it is just as far back as it was going out (unless you are on a loop trail). Judge the amount of daylight left and the amount of time it will take to return. Allow extra time for returning. Remember that some members of the party may be getting tired.

Changes in weather may mean that it is time to turn back or choose a simpler route. Equipment which is not functioning properly (and cannot be repaired) means that it is time to turn back.

Tiredness, sickness or injury in the party are other reasons to turn back. Don't ever continue on the trip, leaving an injured person alone with the idea of picking him up on the way back.

Know when to stop. Signs that it is time to stop may be overlooked because of a desire to go a certain distance or to reach a certain point on the trail. Consider the same points as listed above. Consider, in addition, that it is easier to make camp in the daylight, and days are shorter in winter.

SIMPLE, IMPROVISED REPAIR OF EQUIPMENT

Some ingenuity and the following repair items can usually fix equipment so that you can at least get back on it. Take along:

- nylon cord
- wire (such as mechanic's wire)
- tape (friction or even adhesive tape)
- screwdriver (or a knife that can be used as a screwdriver)

Skis: A commercially-made spare ski tip is handy to have along in case you break a tip. If you do not have a spare tip, use the following emergency repair method:

1. Tape the broken tip back on, lapping the tip under the rest of the ski so it will slide.

2. Cut notches in the edge of the ski and the tip, and tie cord around to hold the two together (lapping as above).

3. Use one shoe lace if there is no cord. (Cut the other lace in half to use in your boots.)

4. Slip an extra mitten or sock over the broken ski end so that the splinters will not catch in the snow with every step.

A broken ski tail can probably be skied on.

Bindings: A lost screw can be replaced with one taken out of the other binding. If you have lost or broken parts, try to improvise a way to hold the boot in with cord, wire or tape, or a combination of these.

Boots: If a sole pulls off or separates, put tape around the top of the boot and the sole.

Poles: Cut a small (½" to ¾" in diameter) branch or pole, such as willow or alder, which is longer than the break in the pole. Tape it alongside the pole in the area of the break. This will not make the pole very strong but the pole will be usable for balance.

2

Technique & Equipment

by Larry Moitozo

Larry Moitozo, the chief contributor to this book and its technical editor, has hiked, climbed, backpacked, cross-country skied and kayaked from Hawaii to Switzerland. He's a certified cross-country ski instructor, developed the Youth Science Institute wilderness program in California, and teaches a wilderness ecology summer course at the University of California in Santa Cruz. He has extensive experience in the California Sierra (including several winter trans-Sierra trips), the Cascades, the Rocky Mountains and Alaska. He spent four years in the Second Second World War as a medic with the US Army.

While ski touring is a relatively safe sport by nature, one can make it even safer by increasing one's proficiency as a skier. This article deals with cross-country ski techniques. Also included are equipment characteristics that may help you in making a selection to fit your own personal needs.

Equipment, of course, is closely tied to safety. The equipment has to do its job and it has to enable you to conserve energy. You cannot, for instance, be lugging around a pack that is so poorly designed, or poorly loaded, that it's going to exhaust you. If you do, you're inviting trouble.

Day Touring with Light Pack—This is perhaps the most common type of ski touring. Packs are usually light (15-lb. size), containing a lunch, medical and survival kit and hobby equipment. You have to make very few modifications in your skiing technique with this size or weight of pack. And there are few travel suggestions except to remind you to exchange the track-breaking chores with others in your party so all can enjoy the view and the trip.

Overnight, or longer, tours (with 20-40 lb. packs)—Heavier packs require some modifications in skiing technique. They may also require slightly different skiing equipment. Most longer tours expose the participants to more and different hazards than single-day tours. For mainly this reason, it is strongly suggested that the *minimum* group size be three.

It is also suggested that on extended tours where the group will be more than a day's travel from a frequently-used road, more than a single tent be used for the group. The reason for this is to give you the option of dividing the group in the event of an emergency. Each group, then, can have the use of a tent.

More careful planning is required with a larger ski-touring group on a longer tour. While it is important to keep pack weight as light as possible, do not eliminate items that are important or essential for the safety and success of your trip. Many overnight tours tend to be leaderless—or at least there is no appointed leader—and considerable discussion may be necessary to determine what is essential and important.

While it may be safe to ski separately if you know the group, it may not be if there are new participants in the group. Keep an eye on the newer members, at least until you know their capabilities. By all means make certain they know the route and the destination of the tour.

If the group has decided to stay together, the pace must be acceptable to all. Faster skiers can carry more weight and perhaps take longer breaks or even short side trips. It also takes extra skill and energy to break trail, so have the speedier skiers use their extra energy doing more trail breaking.

About 30 minutes or so after starting a ski tour, it may be helpful to make an "equipment stop." Often packs need readjusting and boots need re-tying or someone forgot to answer nature's call before starting. You may also want to redistribute the pack weight among the group members.

It may be important to remind yourself and the group that there is usually a time lag when you first begin physical activity before the body can determine your energy requirements. This is why the so-called "warm-up" is helpful before sports competition. In the same manner, if you are at rest and then begin an activity like ski touring, you shouldn't start out at top speed. Instead, start gradually and work up to your top speed. It's a lot more comfortable that way.

Beginners often confuse this time lag with being physically incapable. You often hear this remark: "Gosh, I've just started and I'm already out of breath." The reason they feel that way is because the body hasn't "caught up" with its energy requirements.

PACKS

There are so many kinds of packs that it's impossible to analyze them all here. We will discuss briefly the different categories and relative merits of each category.

Regardless of what type of pack you choose, it should all be the proper size to fit your body. And it should be equipped with a waist strap. A pack that is either too large or too small is impossible to load properly, and the lack of a waist strap will be felt when you get a solid whack behind the head the first time one of those inevitable and unscheduled forward falls occurs. For the same reason, day packs should have a light waist strap.

Packs fall into two main types: framed with an attached bag, and frameless. Included in the frameless type are those with light stretch bars concealed in the pack bag construction. Regardless of the type of pack, it should be well constructed and in *good* condition. Expect to spend from $30 to $60 or more for an adequate pack.

Loading both types of packs: Your center of gravity is about two inches below your navel and, of course, at the center of your body. The most stable place to add more weight on the body would be at this point. But this is obviously impossible. So you have to do the next best thing—get the weight as close to this point as possible. This can only be achieved by keeping the weight as low in the pack and as close to the body as possible. Only a slight modification of the standard skiing position will be needed to obtain good stability with the weight carried in this manner.

On the other hand, it is very difficult to go over those rolling bumps if the pack weight is carried high. You have to keep the forward and backward movement caused by the bumps coordinated with the weight displacement of the pack. This means bending forward and backward from your hips quickly and precisely and over a rather large arc in order to maintain your balance. This is obviously more difficult to do if the weight is carried high.

THE TYPES OF PACKS

Frame Packs: These are usually made from tubular aluminum or aluminum-magnesium alloys. The alloys are stronger and resist bending (which is a consideration, particularly if you fall a lot). Several companies make frames in which the bag can be attached in two places—at the top of the frame and at the bottom. This type of frame is highly desirable.

Some single-position frames can be modified into two-position ones by merely drilling additional holes to accomodate the pack fasteners. For ski touring the cargo bag is attached in the lower position and the sleeping bag is strapped on above. For summer use it's just the opposite.

Frames also vary in width. While wider frames aid in carrying weight closer to the body, they may hinder proper poling by interfering with the backward movement of the arms. The pack bag has side pockets. These also increase the width of the pack. You may choose not to fill these side pockets if you find they interfere with arm movements. Some packs have two side pockets on each side and this gives you the option of filling only the top-most packets.

Frameless packs: These are mostly adaptations of the rucksack. Some designs include light frames or stays that prevent hard objects like stoves or can edges from rubbing on the carrier's back. Some new models use the load, namely a sleeping bag, for the same purpose. Regardless of the design, all frameless packs should be carefully packed to prevent hard objects from injuring the back, particularly during a fall.

Frameless packs are more flexible and some are made to fit the body much like a coat. The flexibility allows for much more freedom of movement. The close fit permits the center of gravity of the pack to be placed quite close to the body. The close fit, however, also creates a heat condition and consequently a perspiration and wetness problem that some ski tourers find objectionable.

Frameless packs or rucksacks with the support stays designed so the cargo or load is self-supporting are generally preferable. Unsupported rucksacks must be packed very carefully and have some provision, like a strap or lacing device, to keep the contents from shifting. Otherwise, hard objects can shift and end up right next to the back. This can make a fall quite painful, if not dangerous.

POLES AND SKIS

Light narrow skis are really fun to speed around on, but they are flimsier and harder to balance on. Wider skis provide greater stability when you're carrying a pack. Since the weight on the skis will be greater when you're carrying a pack, you should also have a ski with more camber.

Cross-country skis are really not so expensive that most people cannot afford two pairs. There are enough models and makes available so a person can choose a ski that's adaptable for speeding around the hills and another ski that's suitable for ski backpacking.

When you're carrying a pack, your poles should be an inch or 1½ inches shorter than for regular touring. Why? The straps of the heavier pack make it difficult to raise your arms as high. In addition, traversing the side of a hill, you will already be required to have one arm higher than the other.

Slipping your hand out of the strap and using only your fingers through it can effectively reduce the pole's length by about three inches. Afficianadoes have been known to put two "handles" on each pole (one strap above the other), thereby creating a pole of two "lengths."

SKIING TECHNIQUE

The main consideration here is dealing with ways of increasing stability. Decreased stability causes one to fall more often, and this wastes a lot of energy (rising from a fall takes a lot more energy than climbing uphill).

People differ in strength and body proportion. Therefore, they need different techniques for getting up after a fall. It's recommended that you develop your own technique. The following suggestions are offered for your use in developing that technique.

The most self-defeating error made when arising from a fall on a slope is failure to get each ski so positioned that it will not slip when you put your weight on it. The technique of getting up after a fall on a slope is to position each ski with the shovel and tail at the same level—or at least near the same level. If you do not do this, you usually fall again because your skis will shoot out from under you as soon as you begin to put your weight on them.

If you fall while traversing, usually your upper body and pack end up downhill from the skis. It's next to impossible to get back up from this position. You must change position so your skis are on the downhill side. This is accomplished by simply rolling onto your back and extending the legs and skis skyward. Then by swinging your legs downhill, while maintaining this position, the body and skis will be in a better position from which to rise. With a little practice the momentum generated by swinging the legs downhill can be used to rise. If the skis do not land with the shovel and tail level, however, the result is most likely to be another fall.

When getting up with a pack on your back, it may be a lot easier to first rise onto the knees. Essentially, this technique allows for getting up in stages rather than all at once. Poles can be use to assist rising after the kneeling position is reached. Crossed poles, flat on the snow and held at the point where they intersect, can be used as a platform on which to push. Poles held vertically in front and pushed firmly into the snow can also aid in rising from the kneeling position

Falls into awkward positions or into deep snow usually require the removal of the backpack before rising. There certainly is little to be gained by long, frantic struggles—only to remove the pack as a last resort. (There are certain unprintable words I've heard some ski tourers use that seem to speed up the process of rising with a fully loaded pack. Such words should be used with caution as they have been known to cause large areas of snow to melt and disappear.)

The technique you develop to get up after a fall should use as little ener-

The Lock-Step Turn: First step, place uphill ski in the new direction.

Place the downhill pole alongside the instep of the boot on the uphill ski.

Bring the downhill ski around (pole will end up between the skis).

The completed turn, after removing pole from between skis.

gy as possible. You can also conserve energy by the way you fall. Falling to one hip with the body uphill requires the least energy expenditure in rising. So if you have any say in the matter, always try to fall in this manner.

INCREASING STABILITY

Side-to-side stability can be improved by increasing the distance (i.e., width) between the skis by an inch or so. Forward-backward stability can be increased by using the Telemark position, in which you extend one foot forward from five to 10 inches.

Please note that the Telemark position reduces side-to-side stability and arms may have a tendency to go upward. Since this upward hand placement results in less stability, the hands should be kept at least below shoulder level. This may take some practice and some concentration to do, but it's essential.

The Telemark position is extremely useful in going over those rolling bumps and dips that are most difficult to negotiate while carrying a heavy pack. The deeper the dip and heavier the pack, the more extension of the Telemark position is required.

SAFE SKIING DOWNHILL

Traverse! Plenty. If too much speed is built up, turn into the hill to slow down.

Struggling downhill on an icy slope with a heavy pack can be dangerous. It's a lot safer to both body and ego to simply take off your skis and walk down.

Dragging poles between the legs on icy slopes requires carefully applied technique, otherwise the pole(s) may break—which isn't too good for the poles, obviously, and may not be good for you.

TRAVERSING UPHILL

Standard traversing technique is all that is required when skiing uphill with a pack. Side-stepping while traversing will, of course, speed up the ascent. Don't neglect the option of side-stepping every other step, or even every third or fourth step. The added increase in elevation is well worthwhile. Traversing more often than usual when carrying a pack is certainly a more sensible approach than changing waxes.

LOCK-STEP TURN

The lock-step turn is much like a kick turn except that it is always done *facing* the hill. It also does not require as extreme muscle extension as does the kick turn.

It's done in the following fashion: As you proceed up the hill and just before the turn is initiated, place the skis about 10 inches apart. Plant the uphill pole right by the heel of the uphill boot. The edge of the pole basket should be three to four inches from the heel. The opposite pole is also firmly planted a foot or so on the downhill side of the opposite ski. Then the uphill ski is raised, tip first, and moved around the uphill pole and securely placed in the new direction. The angle of this new direction needs to be extensive enough so that the tail of the ski clears the other (downhill) ski and the ski won't slide out from under you when you put your weight on it. The downhill pole is now placed alongside the instep of the boot on the uphill ski, and now the downhill ski can be brought around parallel to the uphill ski. The pole that was downhill is now between the skis. This pole must be removed from this position before moving on.

Ski touring technique really has to be developed to fit the individual needs of the skier. The weight of the pack, the kind of pack, the innate coordination of the skier as well as terrain and snow factors all influence the final skiing form.

Using Map and Compass
by Kurt Wehbring

A San Francisco, Calif. consultant, Kurt Wehbring is an enthusiastic and experienced mountain climber and ski tourer.

Travelling in the winter is complicated by the fact that there are fewer landmarks, trails and trail signs visible than in summer. Snow now covers the sign at the roadhead and the well-worn path leading off into the wilderness. In winter, even creeks which were prominent "landmarks" in summer can be covered up and their sounds stilled. So the ski tourer requires more skill, including the ability to use a map and compass, to find his way through the wilderness than does a summer backpacker or hiker.

For the outdoorsman who knows how to use a map and compass, much of the following may be familiar. But a surprisingly large number of summer hikers with several seasons of experience under their belts have only hiked on trails and haven't experienced the adventure of striking off cross-country using only a topographical map and compass as a guide.

Map reading is not difficult to learn, but it does take some practice. Once you get the hang of it, you will be able to picture the terrain just by looking at the map—a flat meadow will stand out where the contour lines are far apart, a pass will be recognizable and the V's that form a gully will be easily differentiated from from those that describe a ridge.

If you are unfamiliar with map reading, perhaps the easiest way to learn is to find a friend who is experienced with maps and have him show you how he navigates. Or if a well-informed friend is not available and you want to teach yourself, pick a popular ski trail where other skiers have made a track or there are markers made for ski touring. Even though the trail is obvious, you can use the map to note where you are and figure out how the map and the countryside line up. If you will carry a map and practice with it each time you go out skiing or hiking—even when the route is obvious—you will soon develop a sense for map reading.

USING TOPOGRAPHICAL MAPS

The topographical maps made by the US Geological Survey are the best maps available in the United States and are available at ski and mountaineering stores as well as the outlets of the USGS (see page 6 for addresses). Most mountain areas are mapped at 1:62,500 (the 15-minute quadrangle) where a mile is approximately one inch, but occasionally the more detailed 7½-minute quadrangle is available. The USGS has index maps by state which are free and a pamphlet whi explains the map symbols. Most of these symbols are obvious, but there are a few of significance to skiers which may not be familiar. The green shading, for example, indicates forested areas. Forests are impenetrable in some regions such as parts of the Northwest and the hemlock thickets near some mountain tops in New England. Often you can check your position when ski touring by noting where you are on the map when you leave a forested area and come into the open. Areas with brush and small growth are shown with random green dots. This might be an area of scrub alder/manzinata or willow, and a place to be avoided if the snow cover is light. Glaciers are indicated by blue contour lines, moraines by small random brown dots, and icefall and crevassed areas by short blue lines.

At the bottom of a topographical map, in addition to the scale, is information concerning the contour interval (usually 80 feet on a 15-minute quadrangle). And below the title in the lower right hand corner is the date when the map was prepared. This date might be significant if new roads have been built in the area recently.

A contour line is an imaginary line which shows areas of equal elevation. The contour lines on your map provide some of the most useful information you will need for finding your way. Areas where the terrain is flat or gently rolling (such as valley bottoms or plateaus) can be picked out by finding where the contour lines are far apart. Contour lines placed closer together indicate steeper terrain. Heavier contour lines, with a figure inserted, indicate key elevations. By checking the figures beside adjacent heavier contour lines, you can determine the direction of slope (up or down).

Frequently you can find your way using just the contour information as a guide. For example, you might follow a valley until it starts slowly rising; then follow the drainage system upwards to a headwall where there is a col or gap between two mountains; and finally drop down into another drainage system and follow it into another valley. At almost any point, even with low visibility, you should be able to know your general location by relating the terrain features to the map.

When you take out your map in the field, it will be easier to relate the countryside to the map if you *orient* the map. This means adjusting the map so that it lies in the same direction as the countryside. To do this, take your compass and place it over the north indicator, which on topographical maps is in the lower left hand corner. Now turn the map and compass simultaneously until the floating needle on the compass lines up with the *magnetic* north arrow on the map.

Once your map is oriented, you will find that the prominent peak on the map is in the same direction in the field, and the same applies with the other landmarks. Lining up the map spares the mind from having to do visual somersaults.

You can also orient your map without a compass by turning it until landmarks and the map line up. This is quick and easy to do and will often suffice if you're taking a general look at your route.

A typical tour might involve crossing a flat valley, climbing up over a ridge and dropping down onto a lake on the other side. From the map you discover that the ridge has a low spot with a prominent peak on the left. In finding your way you should keep an eye on the peak, always keeping it to the left. Even if you should miss the exact low spot on the ridge, you know the general location of your route, and the lake, being a prominent "landmark," will provide a final destination.

To avoid getting lost, perhaps the best approach is to study the route beforehand and then continuously stay aware of the direction in which you are going. A general orientation to the sun (noting that it is generally on the left, for example) will help also. Of course, the sun will move as the day goes along, so keep that in mind.

If you keep in mind which way the terrain is flowing (a long ridge running north and south, a drainage system falling off to the west, and so forth) you can keep on the right track.

On big mountains such as Shasta, Lassen or Rainier, skiers sometimes get confused about which ridge they are on, particularly if they are traversing several ridges. In these cases one has to use care, consulting the map frequently and checking one's location with known landmarks.

One method to keep track of where you are for the descent of a mountain is borrowed from mountaineering expedition technique. Willow wands (tomato stakes available from garden supply stores) are placed in the snow at appropriate intervals—every 300 feet if heavy snow or fog is expected on the ascent. The wands are retrieved on the descent. If there is a crevasse or a sharp turning point, two wands should be used to mark the spot.

TAKING A BEARING

Most of the navigating in the Sierra is done without the more formal use of map and compass which involves taking bearings. But, occasionally there will be times when you will need to find your way using a compass—when there is fog or a snowstorm as there frequently is in the northwest or on the glaciers in Alaska.

A bearing is a line of direction expressed in degrees. If you are heading due north, you are on a bearing of 0 degrees. East is 90 degrees and south is 180 degrees. Since there are 360 degrees in a circle, it follows that there are 360 different bearings.

Let's suppose that you are on the shore of a large lake and skiing to a cabin whose location you know on your map. First draw a line between your location

Using map, compass and two known points to pinpoint where you are. See page 30 for steps in the procedure.

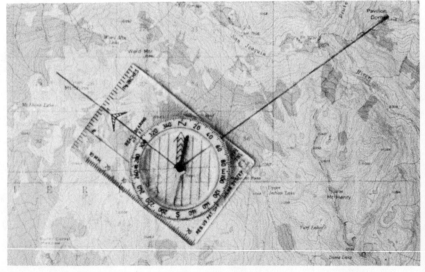

(point A) and the cabin (point B). Place your compass on point A on the map and adjust the compass so that the north on the compass dial is at the top of the map (i.e., north). You can then read the bearing which is where the drawn line crosses the compass.

In order to follow the bearing, take your compass and line up the inscribed north arrow with the floating needle. Next, sight along your compass where the bearing is indicated (say, 32 degrees, which would be roughly in the direction of northeast). On some compasses, such as the Silva, the base plate can be dialed to the bearing mark and after the floating and inscribed north arrows are lined up, you sight along the line which is conveniently marked "read bearing here."

Sighting along the bearing line, pick out an object which is somewhat distant—such as a tree, a rock or a recognizable clump of snow. If fog or snow conditions are severe, you can have your partner walk down the trail in the direction of the bearing using whistle or hand signals to direct him left or right along the bearing line.

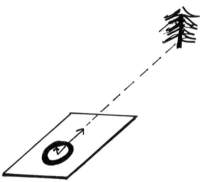

Now ski to the marker object you have picked out and again use your compass to sight along the bearing line. In this way you can continue in a straight line, whereas you might tend to wander off in one direction or another without the benefit of a compass.

If you come to an obstacle such as a crevasse field or open water or a swamp, there are easy techniques to assure that you stay on the same bearing. The simplest is to sight across the obstacle to an identifiable object on the far side and then make your way around the obstacle to that object and pick up where you left off. If you can't see across the obstacle, then subtract 90 degrees from the direction you are going and follow along in that direction *counting your strides*. Then sight along the original bearing and proceed until you are beyond the obstacle. To get back on the original bearing line, add 90 degrees to the original bearing and count off the same number of strides. It sounds complicated, but is easy when you realize you are just doing three sides of a rectangle (see next page).

If you are travelling in an area where there is likely to be low visibility, it is a good idea to take bearings on your course of travel as you move along, recording them in a notebook. Then, assuming you have to travel back in the opposite direction, you can use these bearings as a guide, only now you will have to add 180 degrees to get the correct bearing. Suppose you were travelling due east (90 degrees) along a large, flat glacier on the way to a peak. On the way out you would travel due west or 270 degrees (90 degrees + 180 degrees).

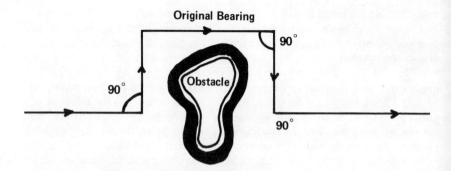

ADJUSTING FOR DECLINATION

At the bottom left on your topographical map is a symbol showing true north (almost always pointing straight up to the top of the map) and the direction of magnetic north with the declination (or deviation) indicated in degrees. Unfortunately, true north and magnetic north are not in the same spot for most mountain areas in the United States. In California magnetic north (which the floating needle on your compass points to) is between 15 and 17 degrees to the east. In order to find the correct direction, an adjustment has to be made for declination.

Failure to make the adjustment can lead you surprisingly far astray in your direction-finding. In an area where the declination is 16° (California, for instance) you'd wind up 1320 feet (a quarter-mile) from your proper route for every mile travelled! If the declination is 8°, you'd be 660 feet (220 yards) out per mile.

There is a jingle about adjusting for declination. However, I can never remember the jingle, so I just figure out the adjustment. If magnetic north is 16 degrees to the east (i.e., +16), when I read a bearing on my map of, say, 90 degrees *true* (i.e., due east on the map with no correction for declination), I have to *subtract* 16 degrees when I use my compass. Before taking a compass bearing, therefore, I subtract 16 degrees from 90 degrees, giving me 74 degrees, and sight along that bearing in using the compass.

In the western part of the United States where the declination is to the east, the rule is: when going from map to the field, *subtract* the declination. Where the declination is to the west, however, as it is in the eastern states, then one would add.

If you have trouble remembering the rule, you can figure out what to do by assuming you want to go due north as shown on the map. It's clear that if you simply followed magnetic north you would be striking off somewhere to the east of your objective. Therefore, a correction by subtracting is needed.

By similar reasoning, when you take a field bearing, such as sighting a near-by peak, and then want to translate that *from the field to the map*, it is necessary to *add* the declination when working in the western United States and the declination is to the east. The rule for the West, therefore, is: from field to map, add declination.

FINDING YOUR LOCATION

If you are skiing along where there is a good view of the surrounding landscape, it is possible to use your map and compass to pinpoint where you are (this is especially helpful if you should become lost). To do this, you must know two

other locations such as peaks or prominent ridges. You can usually pick these off your map by comparing the shape described by the contour lines with what you see.

Here are the steps to finding your location:

1. Take a bearing on a known location (say, a peak).

2. Correct for declination (assuming you're in California, add the declination—since you're going from field to map).

3. Place the compass on the map and draw a line from the known point along the bearing line as corrected for declination. You know that you lie somewhere along that line.

4. Now sight on point B, which is known.

5. Correct for declination.

6. Place the compass on the map and draw a line from the known point B along the bearing line as corrected for declination.

7. The point where the two lines cross is your location. Check for accuracy by noting the topographical features of the map and comparing them to what the terrain around you looks like.

FINDING AN UNKNOWN POINT

Another use of the compass is to locate an unknown peak or other landmark. To do this you have to know your own location. Suppose you have just climbed to the top of a mountain so you know your location. Looking off in the distance you see some other peaks which you can't identify. You can use your map and compass to pinpoint and identify these peaks.

1. Take a bearing on the unknown peak.

2. Correct for declination (going from field to map).

3. On your map draw a bearing line from your known point. The unknown peak will fall somewhere along the bearing line you have drawn. If you're a good judge of distance, you can follow along the line a measured distance corresponding to the distance on the scale at the bottom of the map.

These are the main techniques in using a map and compass: following a bearing, finding your location when you know two points; finding unknown point when you know your location. They are not complicated, but do require some practice.

To keep your memory refreshed, here are the declination rules again:

In the western US (where declination is to the east):

—going from map to field, subtract declination.

—going from field to map, add declination.

In the eastern US (where declination is to the west):

—going from map to field, add declination.

—going from field to map, subtract declination.

(**Editor's note:** While map and compass are best for route-finding, there are situations where the winter traveller can find himself without these items. Compasses can be lost or broken, for instance, and maps can be made useless by water or fire. If you're lost without map and compass, and you decide to try to find your way out to safety, the following suggestions are offered to prevent aimless wandering. Please note that it may be safer to remain where you are and wait for help if: 1) the weather is bad, and/or 2) your group is tired or weak.

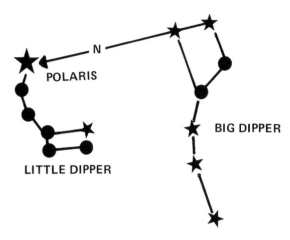

Finding the North Star: Draw an imaginary line through the two stars in the cup of the Big Dipper that are the farthest from the handle. This line will pass out of the constellation through the top of the Dipper's cup. Extend this line for about 2½ times the distance between the two aforementioned stars. The medium-bright star at the end of the extended line will be Polaris, the North Star.

Following a stream: With few exceptions, namely the north slope of Alaska, streams lead to civilization. Because streams often have steep banks, one doesn't need to stay immediately beside the stream. Instead, it's only necessary to stay in reasonable proximity to the drainage system, using only occasional sightings of the stream for reassurance that the route is being followed.

Using a watch as a compass: Follow the directions given on page 15. Make certain your watch is wound and showing the correct time.

Participating in any of the increasingly popular orienteering programs will quickly assist you in becoming expert with map and compass. These programs are fun social events. They are also an excellent means of illustrating the precision as well as the shortcomings of the modern sophisticated compass.)

3

Knowing the Weather

by Ray Hatton

Ray Hatton is associate professor of geography at Central Oregon Community College in Bend, Ore.

A winter excursion into the nation's forests and mountains can be an exhilarating and rewarding experience. The day starts out with a clear sky, a bright sun, and a slight breeze. The great outdoors beckons one and all. However, Mother Nature can be anything but kind and gentle, and many a day, overnight or extended winter excursion has ended in tragedy.

This article is intended to provide the reader with some basic understanding of weather forecasting and weather conditions which may be experienced in winter. My actual experience and familiarity with cold season outdoor activities largely relates to the Cascade Range in central Oregon and to the west coast of America. Other geographical areas—Rockies, Midwest, New England, etc.—will have different climatological factors responsible for winter weather, but many of the weather sequences and occurrences are in many ways similar.

WEATHER FORECASTING

It is often advisable to avoid severe winter weather hazards rather than to deliberately flaunt the elements. The news media—television, radio and newspapers—are handy for checking out weather forecasts. If you live in a metropolitan area, the local weather service office will readily supply you with some basic information. Whatever the source, the information you want should include the expected temperatures (maximum and minimum), wind speed and direction, and the possibility of a storm system moving into the area in which you'll be travelling (its timing, intensity, and possible duration). The existing and the anticipated freezing levels often supplied in television news reports may be of considerable importance.

Driving conditions, possible visibility, protection against snow, a warming or cooling trend are some of the values to knowing freezing levels. However, keep in mind that with a freezing level of 4,000 feet, the snow will probably fall as low as 3,000-3,500 feet.

I have found that television weather maps and reports, when thoroughly analyzed and presented by a competent meteorologist, provide the most accurate weather information. Satellite photographs pick up storm systems often undetected by scattered ground observers. A good weather map may include up-to-date information on temperature extremes, precipitation totals, the location of high and low pressure systems, the intensity of the storms (as shown by isobars—lines of equal pressure on the map). Many metropolitan newspapers include detailed weather maps and regional forecasts.

Keep in mind, however, the time lag between when you read the newspaper and when it was set up and printed. Usually radio weather forecasts are continually updated and any changes announced. Once you have left home, the radio is perhaps your last clue to weather changes, other than what you can forecast yourself.

Some warning and cautions regarding placing absolute faith on the above sources of weather information is necessary. The atmosphere is in a constant state of flux. Weather systems, highs and lows, cold and warm fronts, are not always consistent in their direction and speed of movement. Furthermore, forecasts for sparsely populated areas are often vague, at best. This in part is due to the extreme local variability of temperatures and precipitation in areas like the Rockies, and the Cascades. Storm systems in the United States usually move from west to east. However, many times I have been informed of a storm heading for British Columbia which, for some reason, cuts across Oregon.

In winter, storm systems move at 20-30 mph. Thus a storm detected in the Pacific 1,000 miles off the coast of Northern California could move inland within 30 hours. Cold waves seeping out of Canada into the Midwest often take a day before they affect the eastern states.

Yet one other caution on weather forecasting: do not rely too much on long-range forecasts (those 2-3 days in advance) unless a well-established weather pattern has emerged. For example, several days of fair weather may result from a firmly entrenched high pressure system. The Jet Stream (high velocity winds in the upper atmosphere) may steer a succession of storms towards a particular area for several consecutive days.

AMATEUR WEATHER FORECASTING

The home barometer can at times be a useful guide to probable weather conditions for the immediate future. In general, a rising barometric pressure is indicative of "improving" weather, a decline in the barometric reading often reflects deteriorating weather. However, there are exceptions. Furthermore, there is a great deal of personal subjectivity as to what constitutes "favorable" or "unfavorable" weather.

Out in the field there are nature's signs of weather changes. Look for the following signs in identifying approaching storms:

WARM FRONT APPROACHING

In general, clouds become progressively lower in the sky. *Cirrus* clouds (white fibrous clouds—"mares tails") are often the first clouds to appear in advance of an approaching storm. These high clouds, composed of ice crystals, may then be followed by *cirrostratus* clouds. A whitish veil, too thin to mask the sun, spreads over the sky. The sun may then wear a halo, which is the result of the

Cloud Types

Cirrus with Cumulus below.

Cirrostratus.

Nimbostratus.

Cumulus.

Cumulonimbus.

Cumulus Congestus.

sun's rays passing through ice crystals. The Zuni Indians have a saying: "When the sun is in his house, it will rain soon."

The cloud deck lowers. *Altostratus* clouds—a grayish or bluish uniform veil slightly striated or having a fibrous structure—spreads over the sky. These are middle clouds, obscuring the sun. The air then may become more humid and warmer. The presence of dark heavy *nimbostratus* clouds is indicative of steady precipitation and reduced visibility. Precipitation from a warm front is likely to be quite widespread and more prolonged than that from a cold front. The exact type of precipitation, of course, depends on the freezing levels of the air mass at different locations.

COLD FRONT

There may be little or no warning of a cold front approaching. However, its presence is easily detected. The air suddenly chills. As the front passes, winds may move from the south or southwest to the northwest. Clouds with vertical development—*cumulus* or *cumulonimbus*—may follow *altostratus* or *altocumulus* clouds. Precipitation associated with a cold front is likely to be more local compared with a warm front. It is usually quite heavy and intense but of shorter duration. In mountain areas, instability of the cold air mass behind the front is caused as the air rises over the mountains. Furthermore, cloudiness and blustery showers, often snow, may last for a day or two. At the same time, adjacent lowlands may be experiencing sunny spells.

In summary, some generalized cloud indications of approaching bad weather in winter include the following:

1. Isolated high cloud patches thicken, increase and lower.
2. Fast-moving clouds thicken and lower.
3. A line of middle clouds darken the western horizon.
4. Isolated roll clouds fuse into sheet-like forms and lower.

Indications for good weather are:

1. Fog dissipating before noon.
2. Clouds decrease in number steadily.
3. Cloud bases become higher.
4. A fibrous, stratiform cloud wrinkles up and shows increasing breaks in the overcast.

EXPERIENCING WINTER WEATHER

Weather hazards during winter months are varied and many. Brilliant sunshine reflecting from newly fallen snow creates a glare which necessitates the use of an effective pair of sunglasses to combat snow blindness. Suntan lotion or cream should be used to protect exposed skin from both sun and wind, especially at high altitudes. On cold, sunny days, use the solar radiation to help combat the low temperatures. I've often set up a lunch "camp" facing south and sheltered from a westerly wind. I have spread out a reflective thermal blanket on top of an insulated ground cover and basked in a sun temperature of over 60°F, while the nearby shade reading was under 20°F.

The same clear skies which provide the bright sunshine by day are also conducive to rapid radiational cooling by night. If the air is dry, especially at moderate or higher altitudes, with an accompanying snow cover and light winds, be prepared for extremely frigid temperatures. Of course, the type of air mass covering your area will play a major role in determing minimum temperatures. At sundown the loss of the sun's rays, is immediately sensed. Air temperatures usually nose dive quite quickly at first, then drop more steadily to the night minimum which is likely to occur about sunrise.

It is advisable to set up overnight camps before sunset to take advantage of daylight hours and the sun's rays on clear days. Be sure to note the time of sunset in your geographical area.

Cold air is heavy and dense and has a tendency to descend slopes and settle in low lying areas. Avoid winter camps in valley bottoms.

Wind is often a severe hazard in winter. The wind-chill factor should be well understood by all. Keep in mind that only a slight to moderate wind makes an appreciable effect on how people feel—for example, a wind of 15 mph with an actual air temperature of $20°$ F has an equivalent chill temperature of $-5°$ F. The excessive loss of body heat (hypothermia) created by wind and/or saturated clothing and exhaustion creates a dangerous situation (this is discussed in more detail later in this chapter). This does not necessarily occur at temperatures below freezing. Needless to say, avoid exposed ridges and mountain passes which of ten construct and intensify wind flow.

MOUNTAINOUS AREAS

Thus far we have discussed possible weather conditions in relatively low-altitude areas. Higher elevations present additional hazards. Hiking, snowshoeing or nordic skiing at elevations above 6,000 feet may present acclimatization difficulties to "lowlanders." At about 6, 500 feet, there is a 20-percent reduction in partial pressure of oxygen compared to sea level. This affects some people more than others, and at this or higher altitudes, increased heart rates are experienced, possibly along with tiredness, headache and general discomfort.

The orographic effects of mountains lying at right angles to storm stacks greatly intensifies precipitation totals on windward slopes. For example, in February, 1971, Bend, Oregon (elevation 3,600 feet), received 2.8 inches of snowfall while Santiam Pass (elevation 4,817 feet), only 40 miles to the west, was buried by 121.9 inches of snow in the same month. I could cite numerous other similar examples which demonstrate that all visitors to mountain areas should recognize that lower temperatures, and higher rain or snowfall occur compared to what is experienced at lower elevations.

Furthermore, stronger winds in mountain areas add further hazard for the ill-prepared. Not only are storms in mountain areas often more severe than at lower elevations, but the storms are likely to last longer. Tremendous accumulations of snow have been measured in many mountain weather stations. Crater Lake, Oregon, for example, has recorded 37 inches of snow in 24 hours and 72 inches in three days. Referring to the previous section on weather forecasts, really intense storms should be detected, monitored and avoided.

Mountain weather most of the year in North America is winter-like. Early fall and late spring snowstorms, while invariably less severe than those experienc in winter, often catch many hikers unprepared. Don't be lulled into a false sens of security by recognizing only weather conditions at lower elevation.

In this article we have tried to identify means of detecting and avoiding winter weather hazards. Some basic knowledge of the working of the atmosphere and sound judgement should help ensure a safe winter excursion into the nation's forests and mountains. While clear sparkling skies, invigorating air or different cloud formations which create ever-changing landscapes can help add pleasure to your trips, do not underestimate the potential hazard of expected or unexpected weather changes.

Caught in a Storm?

by Virginia Meissner

Our objective here is not to detail all of the outdoor skills which you might need to use in an emergency survival situation. Skills such as how to dig a snow cave, put up a tent, build a fire when it's raining, or how to light a stubborn gas stove can be learned from other people, from reading, from taking classes and from actual experience. Instead, our objective is to help you understand the basic needs of the body, to help you to think clearly in an emergency, and hopefully to convince you to *always* go prepared.

Some of the things which may cause an emergency situation are severe weather, accident, illness, misjudgment of time or distance, getting lost, and loss or breakage of equipment. While all of these could cause a serious situation, weather is probably one of the greatest dangers to life because of the "wind-chill" and "water-chill" factor which can lead very quickly to hypothermia. Hypothermia is a chilling of the inner core of the body which may come upon a person unsuspectedly and may not be recognized until the person is not thinking clearly enough to help himself.

The sad thing about too many of the tragedies which occur because of severe weather situations is that they need not have occurred if the people involved had gone prepared with a minimum of survival equipment and the knowledge of how to use that equipment and the natural resources around them. Just as first-aid training promotes safety awareness in prevention of accidents, outdoor training emphasizes the importance of preparedness in the prevention of emergency situations.

Even the shortest trip, winter or summer, requires careful planning and thought. Study the area in which you plan to travel. Maps such as the topographic maps published by the US Geological Survey, used in conjunction with national forest and wilderness maps, can tell you a lot about the terrain and distance. Study the maps before you go, and be sure to take them with you. Learn how to use the compass before you go. Talk with people who are familiar with the area where you're going. Don't plan trips that are longer than you or the others in your party are in condition to handle. Consider the amount of skill the party members have in the means of travel. (For example, are they beginning or experienced skiers, etc.) Consider the present weather and the long-range forecast. If the forecast is not favorable, consider postponing the trip until another time or going to another area. Don't be afraid to turn back after you have started if conditions begin to take an unfavorable turn. If the decision is made to proceed under less than favorable conditions, be sure you are prepared for the worst.

When you go, give someone at home the following information (tell someone you can depend on).

1. The area where you're going.
2. The probable route.
3. Names of people going with you.
4. Kind of car and license number.
5. Where the car will be parked.
6. Approximate time of return.

Sign out with the ranger or others in charge of national forest or national park where applicable.

Be sure you can take care of yourself independently—if necessary. Members of the party may become separated or others could become unable to care for themselves. Don't depend upon others for food, warmth, shelter or finding the way.

The feeling one often has on a winter excursion is: "What could possibly happen on a beautiful day like this?" Well, the weather could change. So, always go prepared with a survival kit which will provide these things :

1. Means of protection from the elements.
2. A source of instant energy for the body.
3. Means of carrying and heating water for internal warmth.

Whether this kit contains the bare minimum items or is more elaborate should depend on the time of year, expected duration of the trip, and the weather forecast. You will soon find the things which are necessary and seem to fit your personal needs and preferences.

Some suggestions:
Instant protection from elements:
- Space blanket.
- Tent or tarp.
- Plastic garbage bag.

Source of energy:
- Sugar cubes.
- Candy bars.

Internal warmth:
- Container in which to heat water or melt snow.
- Waterproof matches.
- Fire starters or candle.
- Gas stove .
- Bouillon cubes, tea bags, instant soup.

Other possible contents of the survival kit:
- Map and compass.
- Extra, dry clothing.
- First-aid kit.
- Extra food (to replace body energy and for reserve food in case of delay)
- Pocket knife.
- Whistle.
- Tape, nylon cord, wire.

Problems may result from wind, rain, snow, lightning, lack of visibility, cold, dampness and darkness. Consider the needs of the body for shelter,

warmth, water, and food. Help yourself before the situation becomes so serious
that nothing will help. Recognize the immediate dangers and try to prevent them.

What do you do if you find yourself caught by a severe weather change and
have an emergency situation? The main course of action is to keep your body alive.
Ask yourself realistically: Is it possible to return (or trek out to safety) before
nightfall? If not:

1. Stop, survey the situation.
2. Keep the party together, and stay calm.
3. Check the equipment, extra food, and clothing which people have brought.
4. Look about for the natural resources available to you, such as trees,
   wood, water.
5. Make a plan and carry it out (but be ready to change it if the situation
   requires.)
6. Conserve body heat by putting on extra, dry clothing before you become
   chilled, not after body heat is lost. (Being dry is *extremely* important.)
7. Find shelter and make camp. There may be a protected spot, out of the
   wind, behind a ridge, behind rocks, or in the trees. Dig a snow trench,
   or snow cave, put up the tent or any combination of things which
   will provide shelter.
8. Observe others in the group for signs of hypothermia.
9. Increase internal warmth by means of warm food or drink; external warmth
   by means of a fire, stove, or body heat from another person.
10. Prepare for darkness. With darkness comes increased cold. Prepare
    shelter. Find a source of water. Gather fuel for fire.
11. Prepare signals for searchers. Smoke, blasts on a whistle or making other
    unusual noises in series of threes (the universal distress signal) is effective.
    Use flags, ski poles, skis, etc., to mark where you are.
12. Settle in and sit out the storm until there is a break in the weather
    and you can proceed safely, or until a rescue party comes.

Suggested reading:

  Hypothermia: Killer of the Unprepared, by Theodore G. Lathrop, M.D.,
Mazamas, 1970, 909 N.W. 19th Ave., Portland, Oregon 97209

  Frostbite, by Bradford Washburn, Museum of Science, 1963, Boston,
Massachusetts.

  Wilderness Emergency, by Gene Fear, Survival Education Assoc., 1972,
9035 Golden Given Rd., Tacoma, Washington. 98443.

  Any of the many good books available now about the skills of snow camping, ski touring, wilderness survival and outdoor education.

Avalanche Safety

by Larry Moitozo

If I were to tell you that I had discovered a substance that can behave like a gas, a liquid and a solid—*all at the same time*—you might think me a bit strange! But that's exactly what snow does during most avalanches. It floats and disperses in the air like a gas, flows like water, and, in the underlying layers of the avalanche it has nearly the density of ice.

Snow, of course, comes in many varieties—so many that Eskimos have over a hundred names for the different types of snow. Also, the moment a snow crystal forms it begins to change or metamorphose. No wonder cross-country skiers sometimes have trouble selecting the right wax to match the snow condition!

It is difficult to get the experts to provide us with reasons for avalanches. It's easy, however, to understand the phenomena of "angle of repose," which is basic to the flow pattern of any granular material, including snow. Angle of repose means that any granular material will form a cone when poured onto a flat surface. The angle of repose will remain the same until something happens to change the nature of the material. When the conditions that caused the angle in first place change, the angle of repose will change. If the angle flattens, the material will flow downward(the base of a cone obviously has to spread if the peak of the cone is lowered). Anything that will decrease the angle of repose of snow can cause an avalanche. Combine this with the transient nature of snow and you have a really complex situation.

We have a great deal of knowledge, mostly empirical, about the conditions and situations that increase the possibility of avalanches. Unfortunately, this information doesn't provide us with any hard and fast rules—some avalanches have occurred with none of the usual preconditions evident. The fact is that no one can predict with certainty the occurrence of an avalanche. The only sure guarantee against getting caught in one is to stay away from avalanche hazard areas (in other words, the mountains). The next best thing—if you're one of the many people who are drawn to the mountains in winter to ski, snowshoe, climb, etc.—is to have some basic knowledge about avalanches and avalanche safety.

CONDITIONS THAT MAY INCREASE AVALANCHE HAZARD

Snow Storms: Almost 80% of all avalanches occur right after a storm. Even light storms can appreciably increase the hazard, particularly if they stack up the snow at a fast rate. Snow falling at the rate of about an inch per hour creates a dangerous avalanche situation. Storms in which there's a drastic temperature change also increase the avalanche danger.

Snow types: According to a technical classification, there are 10 different types of snow crystals. The smaller dry, light crystals tend to form snow masses that flow more easily than heavy wet crystals. The lighter avalanches are less lethal, though, than the heavy wet ones.

Moisture Content: Any condition causing the settled snow to become more moist can set off an avalanche. Warm wind, sunshine, warm air from a warm front rain, even warm clouds can increase the moisture in the snow mass and cause a very dangerous avalanche.

Changes in Weather Conditions: Cold or warm snaps can cause a temperature differential to develop in the snow mass. This temperature differential can cause either fracturing (usually from the cold) or lubrication of layers of snow (from heat), and start an avalanche. The sudden change, if accompanied by wind, can trigger avalanches by the dozens in some areas. If the wind has created a slab by compressing the snow, and when a weather change causes the slab to break—usually with a loud bang—the resultant avalanches are very spectacular, and very dangerous. Slab avalanches have tremendous power and can travel unbelievably long distances.

SIGNS OF IMPENDING AVALANCHE HAZARD

If you see or hear a distant avalanche, or see the fresh "track" of an avalanche, be wary, for avalanches are obviously occurring. Spontaneous "sunballs" or "cartwheels" also indicate changing angles of repose of the snow mass. If the above signs of instability appear, it is best to re-route your path. Incidentally, it is folly to "test" a possible avalanche area by throwing rocks or snowballs. They are too small a force to give you any sort of reliable information.

Avalanches tend to happen in the same place year after year. Trees pushed over in the same direction usually indicate an avalanche path. Unfortunately, the trees are usually buried during the winter—particularly during years of heavy snowfall. In addition, during years of aberrant snow conditions or unusually heavy snowfalls, avalanches may take new paths.

TOPOGRAPHICAL FEATURES AS THE INFLUENCE

Slopes of from 30° to 45° produce the most avalanches, although avalanches can occur on slopes with angles as low as 25°. Such avalanches are unusual and quite wet. The diagram below illustrates the frequency and angle of slope.

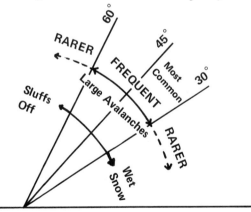

The profile of the slope may be much more critical than the angle. Gravity is continually pulling the snow mass downward on any slope. Where there is a convex face, the snow at the surface has to flow faster than the underlying layers (see illustration, next page). Consequently, tension is created on the surface of the snow. Many times the tension is increased by weather conditions, particularly wind. The surface of the snow then acts like a tight "skin." If the tension becomes too great, the "skin" will break, releasing a sudden avalanche. Because of the tension and the support it gives to the snow mass, these avalanches can occur

on short slopes as well as long ones. As mentioned earlier, they usually are announced by a loud, deep noise.

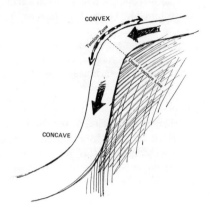

The directional exposure also contributes to avalanches. While the following is generally true, no hard and fast rule that would be useful to your survival
can be drawn. Basically, slopes facing north are colder and the snow on them is
likely to be drier and lighter. This usually causes them to avalanche in drier conditions and to descend more frequently in mid-winter. Slopes protected from the
wind are apt to cornice at the top. Crossing on the leeward (protected) side is
much more hazardous than crossing on the windward side where the snow is com-
pacted and usually not as deep. Slopes with a southern exposure are usually more
dangerous during warmer periods, such as the spring. Wet avalanches are very
heavy and quickly kill people who are caught by them.

The ground cover and surface texture also influence the flow of snow masses. Trees, large rocks, talus (fallen rocks) all serve to anchor snow and during
years of normal snowfall usually offer protection against avalanches. But during
years of extremely high snowfall, these land features may offer little or no protection.

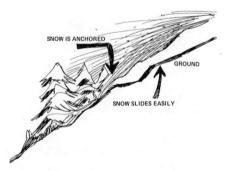

AVOIDING AVALANCHES

With careful route selection you can travel with comparative safety through
avalanche country. However, avalanches are unpredictable and have caught even

the most expert traveller. They can go around corners and even uphill and they can often travel unbelievable distances at very high speed.

By far the safest route across a hazardous slope is above the potential avalanche path (see illustration). Cross the slope as high as possible—on the ridge if you can. There is *absolutely* no logical reason to cross a potential avalanche path if there is another way through.

Many slopes appear to rise directly up to the ridge or the top of the mountain. But there is often a shelf (known as a cirque) just below the ridge. The outer shoulder of the cirque often affords the safest passage.

SUGGESTED PROCEDURE FOR CROSSING AVALANCHE PATHS

If the terrain is such that you have no alternative but to cross a potential avalanche path, the following procedure is strongly suggested:

Cross one at a time! The other members of the party should remain quiet *and* watch the person crossing. This is vitally important! If the person crossing should happen to be caught by an avalanche, it is the obligation of the others to note where the victim was last seen. The search should begin at that spot and proceed down the slope. (Incidentally, when I say that the other members of the party should watch the person crossing, I mean *all* members of the party—those who have crossed the potential avalanche path and those who are still waiting to cross. Obviously, if you can get a double bearing on where the victim was last seen, he may be found much quicker.)

Cross the hazard prepared to throw all your gear off. Before starting across you should loosen the waist strap of your pack but tuck the strap into your pack. Release any safety straps but tuck them into your bindings or boot tops. Remove your hands from the ski pole straps, zip up your parka, and make certain the wrist straps on your gloves are secured.

Use an avalanche cord! This is a simple procedure which can save your life. An avalanche cord is a piece of light 550 cord, about 25 meters long, that a person ties around the waist. Ready-made avalanche cords are colored red and have small metal pieces firmly cinched to the cord that indicate the direction and distance to the person. If you're going to make your own cord it should also be red—for better visibility. Home-made models usually have an overhand knot followed by figure-eight knots at intervals of about a meter. The overhand knots are on the

half of the cord nearest the person. If you wear an avalanche cord, make certain you have the right end of the cord around your waist.

(**N.B.** The cord is not meant to be used to pull you out of the avalanche, but to indicate your location when or if you happen to be buried. An avalanche cord tends to ride to the surface of the flow while the wearer may be buried.)

If you are going into avalanche country, it is also important to carry sectional avalanche probes. While ski poles can be used they are seldom of sufficient length (see section on probing).

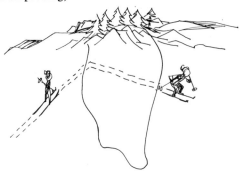

Cross the slope quickly: It's better to cross at a slight downward angle than to cross upward. Don't traverse back and forth across the slope. Most avalanches that bury people are started by the people themselves.

Use terrain features: Take advantage of rock outcroppings and trees or other vegetation. These usually indicate more stable snow conditions.

Cross high: As mentioned before, crossing a slope high and near the top is safer. There is usually less snow at the top, and in the event of an avalanche, the inertia of the snow mass will be far less near the top of the slope than in the lower section.

SNOW IS DEPOSITED ON LEEWARD
SLOPE AND FORMS SLABS

Minimize the danger: Wet avalanches are more dangerous than dry ones. Cold mornings increase the stability of wet snow. Avoid steep, open gullies. Keep an eye open for "sunballs" or "cartwheels." If you're travelling along a ridge, don't accidentally go out over a cornice. Keep to the windward side of the ridge.

A snow cornice like this one in California's Sierra Nevada can mean disaster to the unwary mountain traveller. (Paul Emerson photo).

SURVIVING AN AVALANCHE

If you're on skis and you see an avalanche coming, you may be able to out-
ski it. Ski diagonally (i.e., slightly downhill) toward the nearest edge of the avalanc
When you get caught, get rid of all the equipment that you previously loosened.
Use swimming motions to stay on top of the snow. This is much simpler to do in
a dry, light avalanche than in a wet, heavy one. When you finally stop (or before,
if possible), put your hands over your face and push the snow away. The object
is to get some air space. There is plenty of oxygen in soft snow and you can survive a burial in such snow a very long time. Most avalanche victims choke on the
snow. Now for the most difficult task of all if you become buried—*remain calm!*
This takes a lot of concentration but is your only hope. Panic will quickly exhaust you. The above is summarized so you can commit it to memory:

- Get rid of your equipment.
- Swim to the top.
- Create an air space for yourself.
- Don't panic.

It is possible to extricate yourself from a snow burial. In fact, several foreign countries require mountain guides and ski touring instructors to be able to do
this for certification. Digging oneself out of the snow takes a great deal of willpowe
and experience. The procedure for learning to do this is to bury a person one foot
under the snow, then two feet, then three feet and finally four feet. You can hear
a person shouting through four feet of snow and if the buried person's associates
are standing by, they will be able to quickly uncover him if he should panic.

IF YOU ARE THE SOLE SURVIVOR

Stay at the scene: You alone are the victim's best chance for survival. Don't
leave him unless you're *positive* help is only a short time away. If you decide to
run for help, mark the spot where you last saw the victim. If you don't, you may
find that when you return the excitement and the time lapse have created uncer-
tainty. If you are considering running for help, remember that a search party
will have to be organized, and this may take an indeterminate length of time. Run
ning for help is seldom the best choice.

Start to search immediately: Follow the avalanche cord and recover the
victim. If the person wasn't wearing a cord, search for signs of the body. Packs,
gear or skis may give you hints on where to look. Listen for sounds. When first
buried, the victim may shout. (Incidentally, continual shouting will bring on exhaustion quickly, and if a person is deeply buried, the shouts may not be heard
anyway.)

*Probe pattern in searching for a person
buried by avalanche.* Probing should
start at the point where the victim was
last seen and then "fan out" down the
slope.

Probe: Use your ski pole upside down for a probe. If you have carried a sectional probe, you'll be able to probe deeper. Insert the probe at approximately
one foot intervals in the snow and use the suggested search pattern (see illustration), beginning at the spot where you last saw the individual. After an hour of

searching, the victim only has a 50% statistical chance of survival. But you can do a lot of searching in one hour.

WHEN YOU FIND THE VICTIM

Look for vital signs: Breathing may have ceased. Open the mouth and clear it of any snow or debris. Immediately start mouth-to-mouth artificial respiration. (See instructions on pages 72 and 73). Resuscitation procedures should be begun if all signs of breathing and heart beat are absent.

Treat for shock: After prolonged burial in the snow the person is likely to be close to hypothermia. If this is the case, then the treatment specified for hypothermia should be administered.

The Danger of Frostbite

by Sue Turner

Frostbite is an actual freezing of the skin and underlying tissues, usually at the extremities or other exposed areas (example: feet, hands, nose, ears, cheeks, etc.). Damage to the tissue is a result of the interruption of blow flow in the area and formation of ice crystals between the cells.

Understanding the process by which frostbite occurs is simple when one considers that the body's defense mechanism against cold is chiefly concerned with maintaining the body core temperature. When a part of the body—a hand, for instance— is subjected to extreme cold, the cold defense mechanism is triggered. The surface vessels in the hand are constricted, and blood circulation to the area is lessened or completely interrupted. This reduced circulation means less body heat will be lost; unfortunately, it also means the hand will freeze if subjected to the cold long enough. In other words, given the choice between a frozen limb and a lowering of the body core temperature, the body will sacrifice the limb.

The above, of course, is a simplified explanation. In more detailed physiological terms the same process can be explained in this way: Normally, blood moving through the circulatory system passes through the arteries into arterioles. The arterioles branch out into the networks of capillary beds. The blood can pass through the capillary walls, yielding its nutrients to the tissue cells. The capillaries are the only place in the circulatory system where the blood can actually nourish the tissues. After being depleted of oxygen and other substances, the blood returns to the capillaries and thence to the venule, the smaller counterpart of the vein.

In instances where the capillary bed is endangered in some way, in this case, by exposure to extreme cold, blood is shunted through a small vessel leading directly from the arteriole to the venule, bypassing the capillaries. The shunting of blood is not continuous, but cyclical, causing the area to chill and warm in surges. When the blood does circulate through the capillary bed in the cold subjected area, it returns to the heart greatly chilled. If this continues to the point where the loss of general body heat begins to exceed the individual's heat-producing abil ty, the circulation will shut down entirely in the area and allow it to freeze rather than allow the body core temperature to drop any further.

As the tissue freezes, it appears, according to recent research, that ice crystals form between the cells. Evidently, the crystals in themselves do not cause tissue damage, but they grow by drawing water from the nearby cells. The dehydration of these cells destroys their internal chemical balance, causing the death of the cells and severe damage to the tissue.

CAUSES OF FROSTBITE

Actual contact with an intensely cold object is a primary cause of frostbite. One of the worst instances of this is touching cold metal with wet or damp hands. Metal is an excellent conductor of heat, and will draw warmth from the body almost instantaneously. Combining that effect with dampness will often cement a layer of skin to the metal as well as resulting in frostbite. Spilling gasoline on ba hands will often produce the same effect. Gasoline cools to extremely low temperatures while still remaining liquid; when it touches your skin, it evaporates, pr ducing a further cooling effect. Frostbite from this can be severe.

Usually exposure to cold air *only* doesn't cause frostbite, as air is a poor thermal conductor. But the combination of cold and wind can cause frostbite quickly, since wind carries body heat away rapidly—as does water. Other factors which may increase the chances of frostbite are high altitude, exhaustion, fear, hypoxia and inadequate nourishment. (See section on prevention below.) It has been noted that healthy individuals such as sentries, who are adequately clothed and standing still, rarely get frostbite. The condition, when it occurs, is nearly always related to other factors such as fatigue, accident or being caught ill-prepared in a storm.

Intoxication often leads to frostbite in civilization. Both alcohol and tobac co should be avoided in the winter wilderness because of their effects on the circulatory system. Tobacco constricts the blood vessels, restricting circulation, while alcohol dilates the vessels allowing more blood to get chilled.

PREVENTION

The best ways to prevent frostbite are: 1) be in good condition physically (well-rested and well-fed) before you go into the wilderness; 2) wear good clothing (sufficient for the conditions); and 3) think constantly about ways to minimize exposure. You can lose a great deal of body heat through your head, face and neck, so keep them protected as much as possible. Clothing, especially on hands and feet, should be snug but not tight (areas which are tight or bind you will not keep a layer of heated air next to your skin). It should be ventilated to allow perspiration to escape. Wool garments are particularly useful, since they keep you warm when wet and, strangely enough, the cloth dries from the inside out. Mittens are preferable to gloves in extreme cold, as the fingers are not isolated from each other. If your work requires good dexterity, try to wear a glove temporarily on the working hand and a mitten on the other. Silk gloves may be used when fine work has to be done. Try not to touch metal objects, such as a camera, with your bare hands. Keep extra mittens, socks and insoles in your pack You should change into dry ones whenever you stop after exercise which has caused you to perspire.

Avoid strenuous exercise in extreme cold. Panting or heavy breathing gives off large amounts of heat and moisture (the result of breathing in cold, dry air and breathing out warm, moist air). Heavy breathing chills your whole body and could possibly damage your lung tissues. Once you have been thoroughly chilled (even if you managed to avoid frostbite), it takes several hours of rest and warmth to return your body to normal. When you have been rewarmed, don't go back into the cold too soon.

Eat plenty of good food when you're out in the cold for extended periods of time. Carbohydrates, or sugars and starches, are good for quick energy. They are usually easy to digest, and high in calories. Proteins are also high in calories, but take longer to digest. Fats are usually a good heat-producing food, but they must go through the entire digestive system before they can be assimilated. Also, many people find fats almost impossible to digest while at high altitudes.

Weatherbeaten skin seems to resist frostbite most effectively, so don't try too hard to keep face and hands soft and perfectly clean when living under rough-weather conditions. Reasonably clean is good enough. If you do sustain an injury or get frostbite, keep calm. Feelings of fear and panic generally increase perspiration, which will evaporate causing further chilling and aggravating the injury.

SYMPTOMS

The common occurrences of numbness and blanching of toes, fingers or cheeks are often called frostbite, but should more accurately be called frost-nip. True frostbite always does some damage to the affected tissue.

There are two main categories of frostbite, superficial and deep. These are distinguished only by the depth of frozen tissue and the amount of damage.

In the superficial version, the affected part is white and frozen on the outside, but when pressed gently, it is soft and resilient below the surface. After the area has been rewarmed, it becomes numb, turning a mottled purple, and then swells, with a stinging, burning sensation. This swelling will persist for a few weeks, the length depending on the degree of injury and amount of rest the victim gets. After the swelling subsides, the skin will peel, become red, tender, sensitive to cold and perspire abnormally. There is only minimal, if any, permanent tissue loss, however.

Deep frostbite will originally be hard throughout the entire affected part. Even the bone may be frozen. Deep blisters usually form three days to a week after rewarming. The entire hand or foot will swell, there will be blue, violet or gray discoloration and intense aching and shooting pains. The blisters will eventually blacken and shed, leaving a new layer of raw red skin. In extreme cases of this kind of frostbite, especially when it has not been rewarmed rapidly, the entire area will become blackened and shriveled. It will be inflamed if it has become infected. In these extreme cases, usually some permanent tissue loss will occur, but not always.

TREATMENT

The only type of frostbite which should be treated out on the trail is superficial frost-nip. When sudden blanching and numbness of the skin are noticed, the area may be warmed by the steady pressure of a hand, blowing warm air on the spot, or holding it on the belly or in an armpit. Never rub the area, and especially not with snow.

You should *never* attempt to rewarm actual frostbite on the trail. Once the limb is frozen, an extra two or three hours before it thaws won't cause any additional damage. Partial thawing or thawing with re-freezing is far more injurious to the tissues than leaving the part frozen until proper rewarming can take place in a hospital or base camp. Secondly, if the frozen limb—say a foot—is warmed on the trail, the victim will no longer be able to walk on it and will require a litter or sled. Having to carry or pull the victim out could endanger your whole party.

Upon discovery of the frozen area, get the victim to a good base camp or hospital as soon as possible. When the frostbite victim reaches the camp or hospital, two things should be done immediately. A large container of water should be heated until it is about 108°F—*never higher than 110°F*. While the water is being heated, the patient should be warmed all over as he will have a difficult time maintaining his body heat. Give him hot liquids, put him in a previously warmed sleeping bag or place him in a sleeping bag or under warm covers between two people.

When the water has been heated to the proper temperature (for this you should have a thermometer on hand, or if necessary, test the water with your own hand), strip the frostbitten part and insert it into the container. It should remain there for approximately 20 minutes. Water should be added occasionally to maintain the temperature around 108°. Be careful that the injured part is never exposed to extremely hot water or air. In its numbed condition, it will not be able to sense pain from heat and could easily suffer additional injury.

When rewarming has been completed, cleanse the area thoroughly, using mild soap, boiled water and antiseptic cotton. Dab at it rather than scrub. You must be very gentle to avoid further damage to the tissues. For the same reason, don't use antiseptics containing alcohol.

Keep the patient warm and comfortable until he is completely recovered. The injured part should be exposed to the air as much as possible. If it must be covered, use loose, dry dressings. Support sheets, blankets or sleeping bags off the injury. Pain-killing drugs should not be used in the field unless prescribed by a doctor. Aspirin can be used, however, and will produce few side effects.

Warn the patient about the frostbitten part's appearance. Otherwise, the gruesome appearance of the affected part may come as a great shock. A philosophic acceptance can facilitate healing. Hysterical patients have been known to ask doctors to amputate when it was, in fact, unnecessary. A large amount of injured tissue can be saved if it is left to nature's own healing. The victim should be aware of this and not despair.

Hypothermia: The No. 1 Killer

By Sue Turner

Hypothermia, which, by definition, means a lowering of the body core temperature due to heat being lost faster than it can be produced, is the number one killer of winter outdoor recreationists. Commonly called "exposure" by the news media, hypothermia is particularly dangerous because it can occur when one doesn't expect it. Severe cold, for instance, is not a necessary precondition for hypothermia.

The human body functions normally only within a very narrow internal temperature range. When the *core* temperature goes much above or below the norm (98.6° F), the body regulatory centers are affected. The brain is usually the first to show symptoms, exhibiting slowed reactions and foggy thinking. With further cooling, unconsciousness results. If the body core temperature falls below 98° F there is increased risk of disorganized heart action or actual heart stoppage.

The skin serves as an outer shell to the body, protecting the core from changes in temperature as long as possible. When the skin temperature falls a great deal, however, hands and feet become numb, possibly succumbing to frostbite, and it becomes nearly impossible to perform fine tasks such as lighting a stove. When the skin temperature has dropped to this level, it can't continue to protect the body core for long. Soon the internal temperature will begin to drop as well.

Hypothermia usually results from cold, wet, windy conditions. Other contributing factors can be poor physical condition (not feeling strong, not getting enough rest, being sick before you leave on your tour and not recovering properly), exhaustion, insufficient food intake (not enough calories to keep you moving and maintain heat production), and intake of alcohol and drugs.

Understanding the manner in which the body loses heat and knowing how to dress to avoid heat loss is the best way to guard against hypothermia.

The body cools itself mainly through radiation, the transmission of heat from the skin to the air. The colder the air the greater the radiation. But cold is not as great a danger here as wind. Through radiation, the body warms a thin layer of surrounding air. However, if this warmed air is being blown away by wind as rapidly as it is warmed up, a higher rate of heat loss will result (see windchill chart). Wind also blows through clothing, making its insulating value almost non-existent.

WIND-CHILL CHART
Cooling power of wind expressed as "Equivalent Chill Temperature"

	Actual Air Temperature in °F							
Wind (mph)	40	30	20	10	0	-10	-20	-30
5	35	25	15	5	-5	-15	-25	-35
10	30	15	5	-10	-20	-35	-45	-60
15	25	10	-5	-20	-30	-45	-60	-70
20	20	5	-10	-25	-35	-50	-65	-80
25	15	0	-15	-30	-45	-60	-75	-90
30	10	0	-20	-30	-50	-65	-80	-95
35	10	-5	-20	-35	-50	-65	-80	-100
40	10	-5	-20	-35	-55	-70	-85	-100

Conduction of heat from one material to another also saps heat from the body in cold conditions. Snow, rock and metal are all good conductors of heat, but it is often overlooked that water is an excellent conductor as well. In addition, it lessens the insulating capacity of most clothes. Getting wet can rob you of heat quicker than almost anything else. People who have fallen into extremely cold water, like the Arctic Ocean, have been known to die in 90 seconds! Thus, the first rule of avoiding hypothermia is: *stay dry*.

Care must be taken regarding dampness caused by body perspiration. This is where the so-called layer principle of clothing is so effective. Dressing in layers allows moisture to be absorbed by the inner layers without affecting the insulating capacities of the outer layers. And when these inner layers, such as fish-net underwear or a cotton T-shirt, become damp they can be easily changed for dry ones. Layers of clothing also enable you to adjust for various temperatures and levels of activity. When exercising heavily, you may want to wear only a T-shirt and a sweater. Stopping for lunch will probably call for adding a parka and perhaps another sweater.

SYMPTOMS

How can you tell when you or someone in your group is developing hypothermia? Many of the early symptoms are ignored by most people, but spotting the symptoms early and taking quick action will prevent potential disasters. The first noticeable signs are usually intense shivering, tension in the muscles, fatigue, and a feeling of deep cold or numbness. Probably sounds familiar, doesn't it? Many of us have experienced these symptoms. When we have, we usually headed for the nearest lodge or warming room. But sometimes there is no lodge to duck into to get rewarmed. Or perhaps you choose to ignore the symptoms because it's "too good a day to go indoors."

What happens next, unless some steps are taken to halt the body heat loss, is that the symptoms will become more pronounced. You may exhibit poor coordination, stumble more frequently, and slow your pace. You may also have some difficulty articulating when you talk. These symptoms are usually noticeable to your companions, if not to you. They should take immediate steps to warm you up. Without warming, the symptons can worsen until death occurs.

PREVENTION

Hypothermia is more easily prevented than treated. When out in the cold, you should always beware of the possibility of hypothermia and what you can do to prevent it. In the first place, never overestimate your ability to withstand cold. It is very difficult to predict in what ways the weather will change or what little accidents may unexpectedly keep you out overnight. Wear and carry clothing which can be added and subtracted in layers.

Keep in mind the all-important factors of warmth, dryness, and wind- and water-proofing. Include wool garments whenever possible. Wool is one of the best insulating fibers known to man, and is the only one which retains most of its insulation when wet. Goose down is generally recognized as an excellent insulator, but it loses its insulating qualities almost entirely when wet. You should also have wind- and waterproof (or resistant) clothing, such as a 60-40 parka (one made of cloth which is 60% cotton, 40% nylon) and rain chaps. Keep your head and neck covered. Carry extra, dry garments for the entire body, but particularly for your head, neck, feet and hands.

To keep your energy production high, have a good supply of food with you. Eat your meals on schedule and nibble between meals for a continuous supply of energy. Candy and dried fruits are good for quick energy, while nuts and other proteins and fats have a slower but more long-lasting effect.

Carry an emergency shelter with you, such as a tube tent, or a strong, water-proof tarp. If the weather turns bad when you are out on the trail, you will be able to set up an emergency camp until the weather improves enough for you to travel. In the event of a storm it is important to stop and set up camp early. Going on in a cold, snowy blizzard may likely bring on the early symptoms of hypothermia, threatening your judgement and hand-eye coordination. Your lessened capabilities will make it difficult to perform routine tasks when you do stop. You might not be able to light your stove, let alone choose the best campsite and set up a tent.

Finally, keep active after you settle in. An emergency shelter is not likely to be as cozy as a base camp, so it is necessary to help your muscles produce heat. Isometric exercises have been shown to be very effective for this purpose. You can do them in a confined area (such as a sleeping bag or tent), and they do not expose you to additional cold through violent motions. Isometric exercises can be done by pitting opposing muscles against each other or simply contracting the desired muscles, holding for a few seconds and then relaxing. In this way you can systematically exercise the whole body.

TREATMENT

The treatment for hypothermia is basically very simple, although it can be difficult under the circumstances in which hypothermia occurs. A person suffering from hypothermia is losing heat at a rate faster than he can produce it. First of all, therefore, you must reduce his rate of heat loss. Bring him out of the elements, putting him in your tent or some other type of shelter. Make sure that he is in some way insulated from the ground. Take off any clothing that might be wet and replace it with dry clothing. You might put windproof and waterproof gear on him. Encourage him to start some isometric exercises if he can.

Reducing or stopping the loss of heat is helpful, but it will not actually restore heat to a severely chilled person. The ideal way to restore body heat is to immerse the hypothermia victim in a tub of warm (108°F) water. However, that is not very practical in most wilderness situations. When you're bivouacked out in the middle of nowhere, the best way to help the victim is to put him into a warm sleeping bag, preferably with another person (also warm). You can give the victim hot drinks and put canteens filled with hot water in the sleeping bag with him. If a sleeping bag or shelter is not available, huddle with the victim in the center of your group, so he can possibly absorb some of your heat.

It can take a long time to warm up completely, so be patient and don't rush the victim into moving before he's ready. He will be susceptible to the cold for quite a while after rewarming and should be aware of this fact.

Preventing Dehydration

by Larry Moitozo

How does one become dehydrated on a winter excursion? The logical answer would seem to be over-exertion and perspiration. However, you can get dehydrated in winter even if you don't over-exert.

Air normally contains a reasonably high proportion of water vapor. The effect of cold, below-freezing temperatures is to remove the water vapor by freezing it. Hence the cold air we breathe is very dry. When this dry air is in our lungs, it warms up above the freezing point and because it was so dry when it was inhaled, it absorbs a lot of moisture. Consequently, we exhale a lot more moisture in winter than we would normally.

The same principle applies regarding the surface of our skin. Since dry air can absorb and hold more moisture, we lose moisture faster from the skin in winter than if we were in a warmer and wetter atmosphere.

The radiant heating from the sun also facilitates moisture loss in winter. Snow, being white and reflective, reflects heat back into bodies or substances which are darker than the snow. When we're outdoors in winter our bodies absorb the heat and this heat causes us to perspire, with this perspiration evaporating and passing off readily into the dry, cold air.

Even the snow can absorb moisture given off from our bodies. Often snow campers awaken in the cold mornings inside their tents to find the inner walls of the tent covered with a fine frost. This frost is simply frozen moisture from the snow campers' bodies and represents only a fraction of the moisture lost by them during the night. The same thing happens when one is in snow caves and shelters, too, but it goes undetected.

PREVENTION OF DEHYDRATION

Much perspiration loss can be avoided by using several layers of lighter clothing rather than a few layers of heavier clothing. By simply removing a layer or two, a person can accurately match the activity level to the temperature and avoid perspiration.

Tanking up!—It's possible to emulate the camel. Slowly drink four to five full cups of water and carry your water in your stomach. Ice cold water should be drunk very slowly to avoid cramp or chill. Preferably, the water should be warmed to about 60°F before drinking.

Canteens can be filled with hot water in the morning and insulated with spare clothing to take with you on your trip. Some find warm water satisfying to drink while others may find it necessary to cool the water with snow to a more satisfactory temperature.

Take full advantage of water sources *whenever* you find them to replenish your body's water supply. Drink when you're thirsty, *and* when you have water available.

Eating snow—While this brings some relief to dry mouths, it is very difficult to satisfy your body's water requirements in this fashion. Since cold, dry snow melts down to about one tenth of its volume in water, it may take 10 cups of snow to make one cup of water.

Becoming thoroughly chilled and still remaining thirsty would be the probable result of attempting to satisfy your thirst by eating snow. Several recent deaths in the snow were accelerated by the victims' attempts to satisfy their thirst in this way.

If you do eat snow, do it only as a "water snack"—and not as a main source of water, and by all means make sure the snow you eat is clean.

Another sometimes-overlooked method of getting water back into the body is by eating food which has extra water added. Making soups, lemonade and gelatin desserts with extra water is excellent for this purpose.

4

Basic Medical Aid

by Larry Moitozo

The purpose of this article is to provide casual winter travellers with the basic knowledge and skill to comfortably deal with most minor medical contingencies. It would be a hopelessly cumbersome task to describe all possible conditions and situations you might encounter. It would also be asking too much of you to memorize all the possible ways to deal with these contingencies. Instead, we are emphasizing skills and general principles with the understanding that your good sense and intelligence will guide you as to their use.

CLEAN AND STERILE

Clean means free from dirt or filth. Sterile means free from living organisms or germs. Obviously, it's going to be very difficult to keep things sterile in the precise sense of the word when you are in the wilderness. However, the wilderness, particularly in winter, is apt to be quite clean. And it's not too difficult to keep things that way.

Most dressings come sterilized. If the packaging and wrappers of these materials are kept unbroken, you, in effect, have sterile materials. The materials most often become contaminated when they are improperly handled. With a little practice (see illustration 1) you can open and apply a dressing without touching the surface which will face the wound.

Your hands are, of course, the most common source of contamination. Before you start to deal with any wound, carefully wash your hands. Your supply kit should contain several towelettes (pre-packaged cleaning tissues that contain detergents and alcohol). These are handy for cleaning hands in the event that water is not available. By the way, make certain you do not drop or leave behind any of the aluminum foil in which the towelettes come wrapped.

DRESSINGS AND BANDAGES

Except where otherwise indicated (see article on serious injury), the wound and the surrounding skin should be carefully cleaned. Use a mild antiseptic for this purpose. If an antiseptic is not available, then a towelette could possibly be used. Any foreign material should also be carefully removed—provided, of course, that no further injury is going to be caused by doing this. While cleaning the skin also remember to clean any tools, forceps or scissors that might come in contact with the general area. When cleaning the area, steady your hands by resting them on the individual on whom you are working. This not only prevents you from "missing," but will alert you if the person makes a sudden movement. If it's impossible to get the wound clean, you might use one of the antibiotic ointments (such as Mycitracin) on the wound before you proceed with the dressing.

Sterile dressings come in a variety of sizes. Your kit (see list at end of this article) should contain 2"x2" and 4"x4" gauze pads. If the wound has any small broken blood vessels, use three, four or more of the appropriately sized dressings. Apply these without touching the side of the gauze that is going to go next to the wound. If you accidentally drop a dressing, discard it and use a fresh one.

The bandage comes next. It serves a variety of purposes. The first is to keep the wound clean. It does this, of course, by keeping the dressings clean. The second is to partially immobilize the area. Immobilization prevents further damage and helps to stop the bleeding.

Applying a bandage is not difficult. The roll should be held in your hand so that the end of the bandage is running out over the fingers and not your thumb (see illustrations). When you must twist the bandage to get it to fit properly, the above is, of course, impossible, and you have to use more caution not to drop the roll.

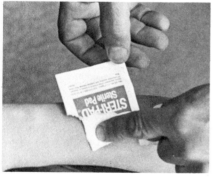

Applying a dressing without touching side facing wound.

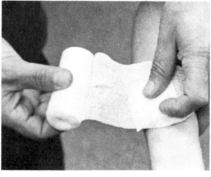

Proper way of holding the roll when applying a bandage.

Start the bandaging by holding the free end of the bandage against the skin, just above the dressing. To apply the bandage, you, of course, use the hand that's not holding the roll. If you begin the bandaging at a slight angle, then you can hold the free end for a couple of wraps, thereby assuring that the bandage will fit properly. And "properly" in this case means tightly enough so it will not slip and yet not so tightly that it will cause restriction to the surface circulation. *A bandage applied too tightly will increase the injured person's susceptibility to frostbite.* This is particularly true in the case of extremeties. (See the paragraphs on severe bleeding, page 62, for exceptions to the above procedure.) If possible, it's advisable to leave the tip of the extremity out of the bandage. This will allow you to check for adequate circulation from time to time.

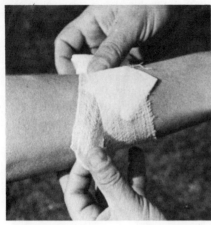
Adjusting tension of the bandage.

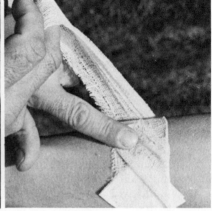
Tucking under the starting end.

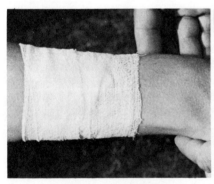
The completed bandage.

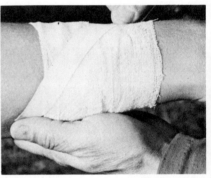
Spiral application of adhesive tape.

After the bandage has been applied, secure the ends with adhesive tape. As illustrated, tape is best applied in a spiral and not in a complete band. The reason for this is simply that the bandage has some stretch but the tape doesn't. If for any reason the area were to swell, the bandage can expand with it, but the tape has no stretch and it may cause loss or at least encumbrance to circulation. Also, if the bandage is applied to an active extremity, the contraction and expansion of the muscles would cause the tape to pull and maybe even move the bandage and dressing.

The spiral can be started on the skin. This will help keep the bandage in place. Don't apply generous amounts of tape to hairy skin or where the skin creases a lot (e.g., elbows, knee area) since removing tape from such areas causes considerable pain.

TAPING A SPRAINED ANKLE

Sprains and severe stretching injuries cannot be differentiated from fractures without the use of an x-ray. But if you decide to tape a sprained ankle, here is a method that is widely used. The foot is held perpendicular to the rest of the leg. If the leg is hairy, then shaving it may be a lesser evil than removing both tape *and* hair later. No strip of tape should form a complete band around the leg. It is often best not to allow a person to walk about on a sprained ankle since it may actually be broken. A sprained ankle will often begin to show signs of healing in two to three days. There is no great haste required for the evacuation in the case of a sprained ankle. Extensive damage, however, can be caused by a person walking or hobbling about on a fractured ankle.

APPLYING BUTTERFLY AND "HAIR" SUTURES

Ready-made butterfly sutures can be bought in most drug stores. They are safe and handy devices for closing shallow skin cuts. Their main function is cosmetic, but they also help to stop the bleeding and reduce the possibility of infection. They should only be used when you are *absolutely certain* there is no foreign material in the wound. If you do close a wound that is highly contaminated or has a foreign body in it, you may cause a deep infection that is difficult and complicated to treat. A deep infection can endanger a whole limb.

If any infection develops in a wound after you have applied a butterfly suture, remove the suture and allow the wound to drain.

Clean cuts to the scalp may be closed with "hair" sutures. Again, make *absolutely certain* that the cut is clean. To apply this type of suture, clean two strands of hair on either side of the cut (using alcohol for this purpose). Carefully tie the two strands together using a square knot. Draw it tightly enough only to close the wound. Keep a close watch on the wound for any sign of infection. These signs include swelling, presence of pus and progressively increasing redness. If any of these signs appear, immediately release the suture and allow the wound to drain.

Large wounds that may involve nerves or tendons should not be closed, but dressed as cleanly as possible and then treated by a physician. Cuts to hands and fingers do not need to be deep for tendons to be severed. The hand is a complicated part of the body with many nerves and tendons fairly close to the surface. Wounds to this part of the body are quite common and any wound that looks even mildly serious should receive the attention of a physician.

Considerable care of the dressed wound is required in winter. The most common hazard is wetness. Water entering a dressing will certainly carry contaminating bacteria with it. Loose wrapping with plastic sheeting may keep out snow, but adequate ventilation must be assured or perspiration may wet the dressing as well. A bandana tied on top of the clothing over the dressing might also be utilized to help keep the dressing dry.

BLISTERS

Wet socks and badly fitted boots are almost guaranteed to create blisters on a ski tour or snowshoe hike. If you can treat the blister before it actually forms, so much the better, but after a blister has formed, the following is suggested:

Clean and dry the foot. Cut a piece of moleskin that will reach at least half an inch in every direction beyond the surface of the blister. Cut a hole through the moleskin the exact size of the blister. To assure the correct size of the hole, try the moleskin over the blister before you remove the plastic backing from the moleskin.

In severely cold weather you may need to heat the adhesive surface of the moleskin in order to make it stick properly. An easy method of heating is with a match. Simply remove the plastic backing and hold the match close to the adhesive surface of the moleskin. It's better to hold the match and the moleskin side by side or the moleskin will get covered with carbon, which will prevent it from adhering properly.

Apply the "doughnut" over the blister, allowing the blister to protrude through the hole. Hold the "doughnut" in place with your hand for a few seconds to insure that the moleskin will stick.

Do not break the blister! If the blister is already broken, another treatment is suggested. Remember that a blister is created by friction and rubbing. What you are attempting to do is build up the area around the blister so there is no further friction on the blister itself, In some cases it may be necessary to use two or three "doughnuts" on top of each other to do the job right.

If the blister has broken, the following is suggested:

Carefully snip off the overlying skin. Use freshly cleaned (with alcohol) scissors and forceps for this procedure. Apply a small dab of antibiotic ointment to the abraded surface, and cover it with a small piece of sterile gauze. Cut the gauze with clean scissors.

Make a "doughnut" as above, but cut the hole sufficiently small so that the edge of the gauze will be held down by the moleskin.

A second "doughnut" may be applied right over the first. It may be helpful to make the hole in the second "doughnut" a bit smaller than the hole in the first one.

Blisters between the toes are treated differently. They, too, are caused by friction. Considerable relief can be obtained by the use of lambs' wool. This is the material that ballet dancers use in the toe of their dancing shoes. It can be obtained from almost any complete drug store.

The idea is to wind the material in between the toes, going alternately over the top and under the toes. This separates the toes from each other. The toes should be carefully cleaned and dried before applying lambs' wool.

The actual technique for using lambs' wool to relieve the discomfort of toe blisters is as follows:

Pull off a strip of lambs' wool about three inches long and approximately a quarter to a half-inch in diameter. The diameter of the strip will depend largely on how much separation between the toes is needed.

After the foot is dry and clean, carefully wind the strip between the toes. Now carefully put on your undersock while taking care not to displace the lambs' wool. Put on your outer sock and try the boot back on your foot.

Readjustment is usually necessary until you learn how much lambs' wool is needed for adequate relief.

Another use for lambs' wool is to modify badly fitting cross-country ski boots so as to make them a little less painful. If your boot is too long and the break in the boot upper is over the toes (in other words, too far forward), then the break will push down on the big toe. This will cause the big toe to be painfully crushed, particularly during one of those awkward forward falls. If lambs' wool is put down into the boot just in front of the big toe, this will help to keep the leather of the boot upper from coming down on top of the toe. Again you have to experiment to determine the amount of lamb's wool necessary to correct the problem. (Absorbent cotton cannot be substituted for lambs' wool. It will compact and will not "rebound" as will lamb's wool.)

SOLAR BURNS

Sun worshippers should spend less time at the beach and much more time in the snowy mountains. Why snowy mountains? As you go higher into the mountains you have less atmosphere; thus, less ultraviolet radiation is filtered out. And the snow will also reflect about 80-90% of the ultraviolet radiation that strikes it. Therefore, you will end up getting about double the dose of sunlight that you get at the beach.

But if you're susceptible to sunburn, you have to be especially careful in the snowy mountains. Lips and eyes need special protection. Noses are often coated with zinc oxide—Labiosan, a special ointment, seems to stick better to lips than zinc oxide. Eyes need to be protected by good sunglasses. Eskimo glasses will do in the event you do not have sunglasses or have lost them. But good dark glasses are a very worthwhile purchase, since the surface of the eye, both the cornea and the white part (conjunctiva), can sunburn just as the skin. The main difference is that you don't feel "eye sunburn" until you have been burned. This condition is called snow-blindness. It doesn't hurt to get but it really hurts to have. The best description of the sensation is that it feels like dry sand under your eye lids.

The treatment for snow-blindness is minimal. It usually cures itself in a few days. Cold compresses may help to reduce the pain. Eye drops, particularly if not prescribed by a physician, are next to useless. Wearing dark glasses and keeping out of the light for a few days is about all you can do. The unusual pain of snow-blindness is sufficient to encourage the victim to purchase a good pair of dark glasses before going out in the snow for any considerable amount of time again.

Regular fire-type burns are not as infrequent in winter time as you might suspect. A lot of winter camping gear is quite flammable. And improper use of gas and/or kerosene stoves can easily result in burns.

As you may already know, burns are classified according to degrees of severity. A first-degree burn involves only the surface of the skin. The damage is superficial and little or no tissue is destroyed. The treatment for first-degree burns is little more than relieving the pain involved. The pain from a first-degree burn can usually be eliminated by merely applying snow. Beware, however, that during very cold weather, frostbite can be caused by too long or too frequent applications of cold snow.

A second-degree burn is one in which there has been destruction of the first layer of skin. Blistering and severe redness characterises this type of burn. Application of cold snow or ice, with the same precautions as for first-degree burns, quickly relieves the pain and reduces the degree of damage. Second-degree burns may require gentle sterile cleaning and the application of a sterile dressing applied over antibiotic ointment (Mycitracin). The function of the ointment is to keep the dressing from sticking to the underlying tissue.

Third-degree burns are destructive to the whole top layer of tissue and sometimes penetrate into the underlying tissues as well (muscles and nerves). Third-degree burns that are more than a couple of centimeters across almost invariably require skin grafts to properly heal. The tissue destruction is so extensive that deep and perhaps deforming scars result.

Second-degree or third-degree burns covering 20% of the body or more are extremely dangerous. They cause shock. Anyone with 20% of their skin surface damaged by second- or third-degree burns must be evacuated as soon as possible. The person will need plasma or blood substitutes and expert medical treatment.

Burns about the face may be particularly dangerous. The victim may have inhaled either the flames or hot gas. This causes internal burns which are very difficult to treat. A person so afflicted must be evacuated with all possible haste. There is little you can do for a person who has burned his respiratory tract, other than placing him in a comfortable position and allowing for drainage of the fluids that collect in the chest.

For simple burns, Mycitracin ointment seems to relieve the pain and promote healing. Complicated burns almost always need to be treated by a physician. Dead tissue and weakened tissue create an area extremely susceptible to infection. The infection may be very difficult to treat.

Winter conditions can cause skin to become chapped and painfully irritated. The cuticles of the hand, for example, often break and cause "hang nails." A light application of toilet lanolin quickly restores the oil to skin and relieves these conditions. One tube of lanolin will last for several winters (and a couple of summers, too). It does not have any water in it and, of course, will not freeze. In colder climates, however, it's a little difficult to get out of the tube.

SEVERE BLEEDING

Severing any of the larger blood vessels of the body results in severe bleeding. Arteries, because they are under higher pressure than veins, present a more complicated situation. The first thing to remember is: don't panic. A little bit of blood can cause a large stain. But remember too, that a severed large artery can spill a lot of blood.

An artery spurts blood with the same rhythm as the heart beat. The deep arteries located in the upper leg (femeral artery) and the arteries of the neck (çarotid artery) are large. (The femoral artery is as big around as your thumb and the carotid as big as your little finger). They are under about 120 mm of mercury (1.9 lbs.) pressure. When either of these is cut they really spurt. The arteries of the upper arms (humeral) are almost spectacular in the manner they spurt blood when cut. Deep wounds in the areas of the arms, legs or neck can severe these large blood vessels and some haste is necessary in stopping the bleeding.

It is not advisable to use a tourniquet to stop bleeding. This is doubly true in winter where cold weather is liable to finish the job that the tourniquet starts— namely, the onset of gangrene. If a limb is deprived of blood supply by a tourniquet, it also becomes extremely susceptible to frostbite or freezing. Frostbite with restricted blood supply will almost assuredly develop into a much more serious condition than a similar problem where there is an adequate blood supply.

The most widely accepted treatment for severe bleeding is pressure over the wound. There is little point in searching for pressure points. The bleeding vessel must be compressed. The best possible place to do this is at the site of the bleeding. Place a sterile or at least clean cloth over the wound and hold it down firmly with your hand. If bleeding persists, pack the wound with sterile gauze or a clean cloth, and bandage the whole area with an elastic bandage. The bandage should be tighter than an ordinary bandage but it should not restrict the entire colateral circulation. If you cannot find a pulse beyond the bandage, or if the limb beyond the bandage becomes cold and bluish, the bandage is too tight and restrictive—loosen it! Keep an eye on the area on the far side of the bandage. The swelling as a result of the tissue damage may cause tightening.

Once you stop the bleeding, it usually stays stopped. Movement of the limb, however, can start it again. Severe bleeding requires care and gentle handling. It may be safer to delay the evacuation of a person with a severed artery for a couple of days. The situation, of course, must be considered in light of what sort of treatment might be needed by the injured person, and what is the nature of the terrain over which the person is to be evacuated.

FEVER

An elevation of body temperature is the most likely sign of an infection somewhere in the body. It may not be possible to tell where the infection is located. Normal body temperature is 98.6°F. This temperature may vary a degree or so, due to physical activity, ambient temperature and so on. The nose, for instance, will carry cold air down the back of the throat and may influence the oral temperature.

Take your time in obtaining a person's temperature in the winter time. The usual three minutes for the thermometer to react is seldom long enough. Get the person out of the wind and into a tent or other protected spot before you attempt to obtain the temperature. If the oral temperature is over 100°F, there may be cause for concern.

When you take the person's temperature, obtain the pulse and breathing rates as well. Immediately start a record of the temperature, and the pulse and breathing rates. Record also the time at which this was done. Describe, too, on paper, what other signs or symptoms you observed. Coughing should be noted, as well as the presence of any pains or areas of discomfort such as sore throat, abdominal cramps, etc. In the event of the illness getting worse, you will have a complete record of both the onset and progress of the illness. This may be of invaluable help later to the physician in treating the person. Be certain you make a record of any drugs, including aspirin, that you have used. If, for any reason, you decide to use any antibiotic drugs, carefully note the dosage and the time they were administered.

The person who is ill can usually tell you what he would like to eat. The liquid intake, however, is more important. Intake of water should be encouraged, and soups can have a little more water added to them to increase the amount of water taken in. Hot Jello, half strength, makes a palatable and healthful drink.

MEDICAL SUPPLIES FOR WINTER TRAVEL

Naturally, the equipment you carry will depend on a lot of considerations: the length of the trip, how well trained you are, how many people are going on the trip and what they're like, etc. What is suggested here is general and has been used by the author for many years. Modify it to fit your own needs.

The table is divided into three columns. The first column names the item. The quantity to be carried is dependent on the size of the group. The quantity given here is for a group of about 20 people (I often lead fairly large groups on backpacking-ski touring trips). The last column gives the accepted use of the item but is not meant as a prescription. Before administering any drug or medication, always read *very carefully* the instructions on the label. Be especially cautious at night and when you are sleepy.

Item	Quantity	Uses
Aspirin (5-grain tablets)	50 tablets	General pain reliever, headache, e
Heavy-duty band-aids (Elastoplast brand is great!)	40 each	Small cuts, dressing for minor ski breaks.
Butterfly sutures	5 large 5 small	Closing small cuts.
Adhesive tape (waterproof) 3-inch roll	1 full roll	Everything from ski repair to medical use to patching holes in dow sleeping bags.
Sterile gauze pads: 4" x 4" " " " 2" x 2"	10 20	Dressings Dressings
Moleskin plaster	1 full can (about 8"x36")	Blisters
(Undil.) Zephiran sol.	3 oz.	All kinds of soaking and skin ster ilization, good for soaking ingrow toe nails and "simple" infections. (Carefully follow directions on la bel.)
Isopropyl Alcohol (70%)	About 8 oz. in plastic bottle	Cleaning and cold "sterilization" of medical tools.
Blistex	1 small 1/8 oz. tube	Lip blister, chapped lips.
Towelettes, containing alcohol and detergent	2 doz.	Cleaning skin.
Roller bandages (new semi-stretch kind are easy to apply properly)	Three 4" rolls Three 2" rolls	The 2" rolls can be cut into two 1" rolls for use on fingers by usin a razor blade or very sharp knife. Make certain the cutting tools are freshly cleaned with alcohol.
Sun screen lotion	4 oz.	
Sunburn ointment (Solarcaine)	3 or 4 oz.	Can also be used on ice burns. (Caused by hard falls on icy hills.)
Elastic bandage	Two 3" rolls	See text.
Triangular bandage	3 per person	Make-shift splints, burn dressings control of severe bleeding.
Oral Fever Thermometer	1	
Scissors (sharp with pointed blade)	1	

Forcep, hemostat-type (with locking handle, useful for many purposes)	1	
Razor blades, single-edge	3	Shaving hair from limbs, removing hair from area of head wound.
Tooth-ache kit	2	Use as directed on package.
Package of Milk of Magnesia (tablets)	1	Tablets preferred over liquid (They won't freeze)
Antibiotic ointment (Mycitracin)	1 oz. tube	Minor cuts and abrasions

Small medical manual.

It might be of real value to carry some prescription drugs. You must have a physician advise you as to their use. The ones I use are as follows:

Item	Quantity	Uses
Tetracycline	one course	Infections. The whole series must be taken once they are started.
Chlortrimeton	at physician's discretion	Allergic reactions and relief from nasal congestion.
Emperine and Codeine	"	Relief of pain.
Opthalmic ointment (eye ointment)	"	Relief of pain from snow blindness.

Treatment For Serious Injury

by Larry Moitozo

For some mysterious reason, accidents in the mountains happen very infrequently. You can spend years travelling about in both summer and winter and encounter only those minor mishaps that are reasonably easy to deal with. You will probably never encounter a major accident of the type described here. But if you do, what you do and how you do it may well mean the difference between life and death for somone—perhaps even a loved one.

When an accident happens there is often a lot of confusion. Hysterical or panicky people may start giving false and alarming information. The injured person is usually not clear about his condition, and the confusion and hysteria around him may only serve to increase his confusion. Rushing up to a bleeding person, looking at the blood, then reeling back in horror while shouting, "Oh, my God!" will not do the victim one single bit of good! It may, in fact, only convince him that he is worse off than he really is. I once witnessed a 10-year-old child go into deep shock from being bitten by a harmless snake—that the child's mother had hysterically judged to be venomous! So you have to "get your act together" before you can be of assistance to the injured.

Winter complicates accidents. Lower temperatures and increased difficulty in getting aid create a serious situation not encountered in summer. If you are not competently trained in first aid, the following paragraphs are very important to you. If you are competently trained, the following is meant only as a reminder, and hopefully will include some information of value as it pertains specifically to winter emergency aid.

If you are the first at the scene of an injury, look quickly but carefully about. Is the injured in any further danger, or can you assist and examine him where he is? If the person must be moved, do it as gently as possible.

Should you decide you have to move the injured person, pick out an appropriate place to move him to before you start. One positive move may be a lot better than two or three indecisive ones. The new location must also provide protection from heat loss, particularly if there is underlying snow.

Since your behaviour around the injured person will convey something of the nature of the situation to him, be careful what you say, even if the victim appears to be unconscious. Your voice could penetrate to the conscious level of the victim.

You'll need to examine the victim to accurately determine the extent of the injury. If he is conscious and lucid, communicate what you are doing. Be reassuring and confident. If you have hysterical people about, you may want to give them jobs away from the injured. (Is this why country doctors always had young husbands boiling all that water when their wives had the first baby?) Setting up a nearby camp might later prove very useful.

Several things to remember before you start to determine the extent of the injury. The injured person may have no accurate sense of the extent of the injury. Also keep in mind that only a little blood can cause a very large stain. A teaspoonful will saturate a handkerchief, and a couple of ounces spilled on the white snow will make it look as if a moose has been slaughtered!

While there are a very large number of specific injuries with specialized treatment, it is beyond the scope of this article to deal with all of them. What this article does instead is describe the signs of severe injuries of the following: head, neck and spine, chest, abdomen,   and fractures of the long bones of the body. It also suggests ways of dealing with these injuries until specially qualified or trained people can take over. Use your own intelligence and discretion as you examine the injured. The following is not meant as a system or procedure for an examination, but only a description of conditions that are considered severe.

After you have prevented the possibility of any further injury occurring, you should immediately determine the condition of the injured person's breathing and heartbeat. If either of these has ceased, steps must immediately be taken to get them started again (see section titled "Resuscitation" later in this article).

HEAD INJURIES

If you put your fingers firmly on your scalp and rub hard, you will get the idea that your scalp is only about an eighth to a quarter of an inch think. In reality, the scalp is from one half to three-quarters of an inch thick—and loaded with blood vessels, so that when it's cut it bleeds profusely. This is true even if the head injury is relatively superficial.

On the other hand, in some head injuries, the scalp may not bleed at all but the brain may be damaged. You will have to look for other signs to determine if brain damage has occurred. These signs and some indications of their significance are as follows:

1. Unconsciousness: The depth of the coma and the duration of unconsciousness are a rough estimate of the degree of damage to the brain. A person rendered unconscious should not be allowed to become active immediately upon regaining consciousness. The person must also be protected from heat loss while unconscious. If you need a source of external heat, canteens filled with warm water can be used as hot water bottles.

Do not leave an unconscious person alone. Left alone for an extended period of time, an unconscious person will usually die, particularly in winter. If the injury is so serious as to be ultimately fatal, the most you can humanely do is be with the victim in his last remaining moments on earth.

Make sure that the unconscious person's breathing passage is open and clear. Do this by opening the mouth and looking inside. Remove any dentures, chewing gum or other foreign material that may be in the mouth or throat. Take care not to push any objects down the throat when you do this. If you need a tool to help remove objects, the handle of a spoon may serve this purpose much better than a thick forefinger.

2. Unevenly or widely dilated pupils of the eyes: Damage to the brain or bleeding inside of the skull can cause unusual eye reactions. Do not allow a person who shows these symptoms to move about and be active. The person is seriously injured—even if he doesn't think so.

3. Unusual or erratic behavior: Everyone will usually act somewhat confused when subjected to a severe blow to the head. If the confusion persists, however, there may be complications. Intelligence orientation is regarded as the highest function of the brain and it's usually the first mental process to show signs of deterioration if the brain is damaged.

Be particularly aware if any of the above signs or conditions worsen. After a blow to the head, repeated lapses of consciousness, distortions of vision or hearing, loss of sensation, or paralysis are to be regarded as damage to the brain.

4. Bleeding from the ears and nose: Make certain the blood from a head injury is from the wound itself. Clear straw colored or weakly colored blood may not really be blood at all but cerebrospinal fluid, and indicates complicated and severe damage to the skull or neck.

Treatment of head injuries: While there is no specific treatment for serious head injuries, there is still much you can do to increase the possibility of recovery. Set up camp and prepare to evacuate the injured. Watch the person carefully and keep track of his vital signs (breathing and heartbeat). Be prepared to administer resuscitation or artificial respiration if either breathing or heartbeat ceases. Make certain that the air passage is kept open. If the injured lapses into unconsciousness, recheck the air passage. Keep the injured warm. Be reassuring. Give him the sense that you care and are doing what is necessary for his survival.

A person who is lapsing into unconsciousness must be constantly watched while he is being evacuated. If the air passage becomes impaired, quick suffocation may result. Severe head injuries almost always require careful evacuation and ultimately the services of a specially trained surgeon. Obviously, however, you can do much to increase the chances of recovery of a person with such an injury.

BACK AND NECK INJURIES

Inside of the vertebral column is the spinal cord. Severe injury to the spine may damage the cord. Such damage may also occur *after* the injury if the victim is improperly handled. Damage to the spinal cord is almost always permanent.

Deep pain and swelling along the spine and neck after a severe fall or blow should be checked for other signs of damage. If any of the signs of fracture are present (see section on fractures), extreme care should be taken in handling the victim.

Signs of spinal cord damage include radiating pains, particularly down the arms or legs, numbness and tingling, and complete or partial paralysis. The absence of these signs, however, doesn't mean that the vertebral column *is not* broken. It may, in fact, be broken while the cord remains undamaged. If the back or neck show any of the signs given for fractures, it's far safer to assume the vertebral column is broken.

A special device called a vertebral frame is ideal for evacuating a person with a suspected vertebral fracture. If such a device is not available, then a wire basket-type litter with firm support is necessary.

Back injuries and neck injuries must be handled extremely gently. If only the bone is broken and not the cord, then the accident is merely unfortunate. If, however, the spinal cord is broken during the evacuation, the unfortunate accident becomes a real tragedy—the resulting paralysis usually being permanent.

PERFORATIONS OF THE CHEST

This is one of the few emergencies where quick and proper treatment is essential for the survival of the victim. A hole through the chest wall permits air to be sucked into the chest cavity. This causes the lungs to collapse and air cannot reach the surfaces of the lungs where oxygen and carbon dioxide are exchanged. The result, if the hole is not closed, is suffocation. Sharp falls onto ice axes or ski poles can cause such a wound.

Treatment: The hole must be tightly closed as soon as possible. This will restore the negative pressure in the lungs so they can inflate and again exchange oxygen for carbon dioxide. The best way to close the hole is with sterile vaseline-

Bandaging procedure to close a perforation of the chest wall. If not closed quickly, such a wound can result in suffocation.

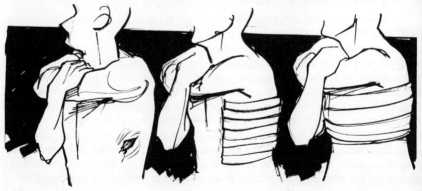

covered gauze. Vaseline and gauze are items seldom found in the average first-aid kit. But most kits do contain some sort of vaseline-like ointment from which a seal-like dressing can be made.

After covering the wound with these materials, carefully cover the whole area with overlapping layers of adhesive tape. A penetrating wound of the chest must be permanently closed by surgery, hence the patient must be evacuated.

A hard blow to the chest may also result in broken ribs. If the damage is minimal enough so the broken rib doesn't penetrate the lung, taping and a few days' rest may be all that is needed. If the damage is extensive and the lung is also damaged, severe breathing difficulty will be experienced (the victim may fight to breathe). This is a serious injury.

Immobilization and using adhesive tape on the fractured area may help the injured get more air. Placing the victim face down and over the injury may also allow for freer breathing. An injury of this sort usually results in fluid accumulating in the lung. Coughing, even though painful, should be encouraged. Even though this type of wound is not as serious as perforations to the chest wall, it is serious enough to require evacuation.

PERFORATIONS OF THE ABDOMINAL WALL

These are extremely serious and will require eventual surgical procedures. When the wall of the abdomen is opened, the whole abdomen is considered contaminated. It is almost certain, too, that when the injury is severe enough to penetrate the abdominal wall, the organs of the abdominal cavity may also be injured.

Treatment: Do not wash or otherwise try to sterilize the wound. If intestines or other organs are protruding, gently and with as clean a technique as possible in field conditions, push them back into the abdominal cavity. Cover the area with sterile gauze. Generously apply long strips of adhesive tape over the gauze. Apply the tape snugly to ensure that the organs do not protrude again.

Evacuation is required and must be done with great gentleness. Shock usually accompanies this injury and must be treated. Also, do not allow the patient to eat or drink *anything.*

FRACTURES OF THE LONG BONES OF THE BODY

The long bones of the body, the femora and humeri (singular, femur and humerus) are very strong. It usually takes a lot of pressure to break these bones. Consequently, their fracture is accompanied by a great deal of tissue damage. This means several things; one thing for certain—there is a lot of pain involved. There is also apt to be a rapid onset of shock. This must be quickly treated (see section on the treatment of shock).

Consideration must also be given to the tissue damage. Pieces of tissue are liberated at the site of the damage and because large blood vessels are close to the long bones and are also likely to be damaged, these pieces of tissue may enter the bloodstream and cause a blockage of blood elsewhere in the body. This is called an embolism (plural emboli). If an embolism occurs in a vital area of the heart, kidney or lungs, the victim now will have two problems with which to contend.

Fractures of any weight-bearing bone or joint are critical and require careful evacuation to a medical facility. The superficial signs of a fracture include: 1) Pain and tenderness at the injury and adjacent to it; 2) Swelling and discoloration—usually red and bluish-purple; 3) Deformation of the limb or the joint involved. Definite diagnosis of hairline fractures, particularly of the ankles and wrists, must be made with the aid of x-ray.

It is not essential to be certain that the bone is fractured. By no means should the limb be twisted to determine if the bone ends grate. This procedure always is shocking to the injured and may release tissue particles into the bloodstream to play havoc elsewhere in the body.

Treatment: The long bones of the body, if fracture is suspected, must be splinted—carefully and adequately. Air splints are easily applied and very adequate. They are not, however, often carried by the causal traveller.

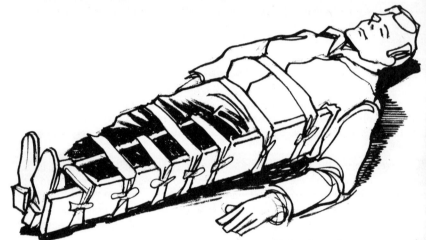

**A broken femur properly
immobilized by a makeshift splint.**

In order to satisfactorily immobilize a fractured bone with a splint, both joints at the ends of the bone must be included in the splint. Any makeshift splint must be carefully padded and constructed to fit the limb—without distorting the limb. The injured person, being in real pain, must be very carefully handled. When you need to adapt the splint to fit the limb, use someone else's limb, compensating, of course, for any size or shape difference. When putting the splint on a limb with a possible fracture, provide support for the limb, and by no means, if it's definitely broken, allow the limb to sag.

In splinting a broken femur, a most shocking and painful procedure, traction to the lower leg must be applied to prevent the bone ends from "chattering together" during the evacuation. If the bone ends over-ride, then more tissue damage will result, the most serious damage being severing of the femoral artery which lies quite close to the femur. Do not remove the boot from the foot. It stabilizes the ankle joint and serves as a firm place to attach the traction device.

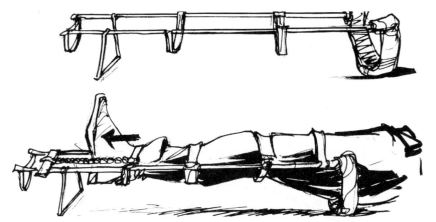

A Thomas leg splint—a sophisticated, time-proven device for splinting a broken femur. Makeshift splints should imitate its function.

A Thomas leg splint (see illustration) is a long-time proven device for splinting a femur. If you use a makeshift splint, imitate the functions of this device. The bar at the top end transfers the upward pressure caused by the traction device to the seat and buttocks of the victim. It also supports the upper end of the splint by transferring some of the upward pressure to the crotch. The crosspiece at the bottom serves to stabilize the ankle and provide a place to secure the traction device.

The pain caused by the fractured bone usually decreases when the splint is in place. Most pain-killers available without the direction of a physician are inadequate. Morphine or Demerol are needed. Both of these drugs should be administered under the direction of a physician.

SHOCK

Shock is a condition caused by a severe drop in blood volume. Blood volume can be influenced by profuse bleeding, loss of blood serum through extensive tissue damage as caused by burns, or extensive infections such as peritonitis. Extreme diarrhea or prolonged thirst can also suffice to reduce blood volume to cause shock. Heart attacks cause shock, not by a drop in blood volume, but by reducing blood flow. It is important, then, to attend to the underlying condition which causes shock. Prompt and anticipatory treatment is the most effective. In other words, shock is more easily and effectively prevented than treated.

Signs of Shock: A person in shock looks sick. He is pale, the skin feels clammy and cold. The lips and fingernails are bluish and cyanotic. The person may be restless and disoriented. The pulse is weak and rapid. The most important sign is low blood pressure. However, the instrument needed to determine low blood pressure, a sphygmomanometer, is rarely available in the wilderness.

Treatment: Treat the cause first. Also, to minimize the effects of shock, the following is suggested:

Place the patient prone if possible. Elevate the feet—unless the legs are injured. At least get the head lower than the rest of the body. It's important to maintain body temperature. This is complicated during the winter. Don't neglect insulating the body from the snow. A sleeping bag may not be adequate if the shock is so severe that the body cannot maintain its own temperature. Substitute canteens of warm water as hot water bottles, or use direct body-to-body contact to provide heat to the shock patient.

Plasma or blood substitutes are eventually necessary to replace the lost blood volume. These are seldom available to the casual winter mountain traveller. Prompt but adequate evacuation is usually the best procedure. You can still, however, help the patient greatly by following the above.

It is also important to exclude stimuli which produce fright in the patient. This would include panic-stricken people and the sight of lots of blood.

RESUSCITATION: ARTIFICIAL RESPIRATION AND CARDIAC MASSAGE

If a person has gone 20 minutes without heartbeat or breathing, attempts at resuscitation are futile. But you often do not know how long it has been. It's not unknown for avalanche victims who look as if they have succumbed to be successfully resuscitated. You have little to lose and much to gain.

Artificial Respiration (mouth-to-mouth system): Check first for a clear air passage. Avalanche victims usually have snow in their mouths. Dentures, particularly partial bridges, must be removed or they may be blown back into the throat. Use the handle of a spoon or even a comb to remove objects that may be forced further back into the throat by your fingers.

Now pull the lower jaw firmly upward using your forefinger, then by inserting your thumb into the mouth, open it. With your other hand, gently pinch the nostrils closed. Place your mouth over the opened lips of the victim and blow gently in. If you blow violently, you may push vomitus or other material that might be farther back in the throat into the lungs.

After the initial breath, and assuming you felt the air enter the lungs, remove your mouth and allow the patient to breath out. Vomitus or other material may be expelled with this initial exhalation. When you're sure the air passage is clear, institute the following: breathe into the victim's mouth at about double your natural volume; repeat the process about 12 to 14 times per minute.

Sometimes air is also blown into the stomach during mouth-to-mouth resuscitation. The sign of this is a distended abdomen after the victim has exhaled. Air trapped in the stomach could cause it to rupture. This is more of a danger in smaller children than in adults.

You can relieve this condition by gently pressing on the abdomen with the flat of your hand when the victim has exhaled. Be cautioned that the contents of the stomach may also be expelled with the trapped air. Before you proceed further, free the air passage of this material.

Following the procedures described above and shown in the illustrations makes it almost impossible not to apply mouth-to-mouth resuscitation correctly. This procedure is by far the most effective way to re-start someone's respiration. The uneasiness one might feel about a victim vomiting while mouth-to-mouth resuscitation was being applied should always be superceded by the serious nature of the situation.

Cardiac Massage: If you cannot detect a pulse at the injured person's neck, wrist or groin, put your ear right against the chest midway between the nipple of the left breast and the middle of the chest. If you cannot hear a heartbeat, begin cardiac massage.

Procedure in applying mouth-to-mouth respiration—1) Tilt victim's head back; 2) Open victim's mouth, make sure his air passage is clear and gently pinch the nostrils closed; 3) Place your mouth over the open lips of the victim and blow in gently.

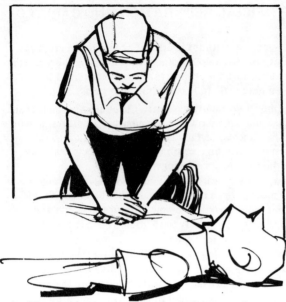

The initial step is to strike the chest a sharp, firm blow, just short of breaking the ribs, using the side of your hand. The blow should be directed at the spot where you initially had your ear. If three or four of these produce no result, then the next step is necessary.

Place the person on his back on a firm surface. Put your hands one on top of the other and place them on the lower end of the sternum (breast bone). Now raise your weight up over the sternum to depress it. The idea is to squeeze the heart between the sternum and the underlying tissues, and thus stimulate it to resume beating.

In applying heart massage, remember that the human body is fragile and you may be overly stimulated by the serious nature of the situation. So be particularly careful not to crush the victim's chest. The chests of young children and elderly people are particularly fragile.

Cardiac massage is particularly tiring—it should have a frequency of about 60 beats per minute. Also, the victim usually isn't breathing, so two people have to be present to keep him alive. Keep checking for resumption of heartbeat as massage progresses. Cease when and if the heart starts beating on its own.

After resuscitation the person must be kept under constant observation. He is usually unconscious for a period of time. His air passage must be kept open at all times. He may relapse and need more resuscitation. Evacuation is always a necessity. The person must be constantly watched during the evacuation for either a relapse or a clogged air passage.

Unsuccessful resuscitation: When to stop? A most difficult question. Artificial respiration should be continued if a person's heart is beating. In the case of cardiac massage, if the heart fails to respond quickly then the victim's chances of survival aren't great. If the massage procedure has been implemented for 30 minutes or so, but the heart has not resumed beating, and the pupils of the eyes are widely dilated and do not respond (by contracting) to light, then the victim is beyond help. Statistically, most attempts at resuscitation fail. However, if you do win, you win a lot, and if you lose, the battle was probably lost before you started.

EVACUATING THE SERIOUSLY INJURED

Evacuating the seriously injured from the wilderness usually means getting some assistance from outside. How this is accomplished may increase the injured person's chances considerably. What sort of message is sent out and what information is included requires careful consideration. The suggestions in the next few paragraphs are not merely light hints, but important procedures designed to increase the injured person's chances for recovery.

When a serious accident or illness occurs in the wilderness, someone must go out for assistance (a good reason for having at least three people in your party). Send the messenger out with a written description of the situation. The message should be dated and signed by the person in charge or by someone who has assumed leadership. The message should include what happened, when it happened, to whom it happened (including the victim's age, address and next of kin), where it happened, an accurate description of the location of the injured person and how this location can be seen from the air. The message should also include the possible diagnosis and what special equipment you might think necessary for the evacuation.

While you are waiting for the evacuation team, sit down and record exactly what you have done to the injured. Include any records of body temperature you might have made, any drugs you may have administered and the dosage and times they were given. Also include any signs or symptoms the injured or ill person might have exhibited. This record may give the attending physician valuable information and it should, of course, be sent out with the injured person when evacuation takes place.

The message which is sent out should be clear and complete *in itself.* After all, the messenger may become injured or otherwise not be able to deliver the message himself. Spending a few minutes, after you have attended to the victim, preparing an accurate, clearly written and legible message may be the most important, lifesaving thing you can do. Evacuation can be an expensive and complicated process. You can do much to facilitate a successful rescue by communicating accurately with the rescue team.

WHOM TO CONTACT

Many winter excursions occur in National Parks. Many of these parks have elaborate check-out systems to keep track of winter travellers. Don't try to fool this system. Doing so is foolish and dangerous.

The National Parks may have their own rescue teams or they may call in outside help. But at least they will know where help is available. In winter, some National Parks, notably Yosemite in California, are posting back-country rangers who have contact via radio with outside facilities and sometimes can get injured people to medical facilities faster than if they were injured in a city.

National Forests are quite different. They do not exist mainly for visitors, and they are, of course, immensely larger. Many of the summer facilities of the National Forests are closed down during the winter and the personnel are on duty elsewhere.

Some areas do have volunteer rescue teams trained in evacuation and their whereabouts are usually known by National Forest personnel. In some areas the county sheriff coordinates rescue operations. It's a good idea to check out whom to contact before you take your winter trip. If in doubt, contact the police. They usually have radio communication with the coordinating authorities.

By no means should you go into the wilderness *without telling anyone.* This is dangerous to do even in the summertime, but it's infinitely more so in the winter.

It is strongly recommended that if you plan to spend a lot of time in the wilderness where assistance is hard to come by, you should prepare yourself with complete emergency aid knowledge. This means enrolling in a good, complete course such as those offered through the extension departments of universities. These courses are taught by physicians or highly-trained paramedical technicians. Some of the courses offer college level credit, and may be well worth your life or someone else's.

A Simple Method of Evacuation

by Larry Moitozo

While evacuating the seriously injured from the wilderness usually means getting some assistance from the outside, there are injuries and situations where a do-it-yourself evacuation may be in the best interests of the victim.

There are many considerations in deciding whether to evacuate the victim yourself or seek assistance. Many of these considerations automatically pop into mind: the seriousness of the injury, the distance to the road head, the nature of the terrain, the strength of the people in the party, and so on. And then there are the "what if's"—what if it should storm, what if the injury turned out to be worse than you thought, what if another injury should occur during the evacuation, etc.

The net result is that only the members of the particular party and their leader (assigned or assumed) can make the decision as to what method should be used to evacuate an injured person. You may find the following suggestions and directions helpful in making a decision. They are based on actual experience. The directions for making the sled were developed from a real situation. The photographs show a replica of a sled used in a six-mile soft-snow and steep-hill evacuation. The injury was minimal; a severely sprained ankle that turned out to be a hairline fracture of an ankle bone.

An often overlooked general consideration is the management of equipment. The injured person's equipment should be evacuated with him. And the gear of the other members of the party should be carried out as well. You might consider redistributing the weight carried by each member of the party as a possible alternative to leaving any equipment behind. If you evacuate all the equipment you also take care of a whole lot of "what ifs." For example, you'll be able to cope with a storm should one arise during the evacuation.

If you decide to leave some gear behind, wrap it up in a bundle and stow it high in a protected spot. It may be a good idea to leave your name and address with the gear to identify it. Don't leave the equipment where it will get covered by snow, or damaged by animals or the weather.

It may be possible to evacuate the injured person by carrying him or her on your back. A simple sling of nylon webbing greatly facilitates this. Tie about 10 feet of one-inch nylon webbing in a loop and place it over your shoulders, behind your neck and extending downward under your arms to make two loops for the injured person's legs.

If your party is on snowshoes, you will probably end up carrying the injured person out on a litter. The addition of shoulder straps makes the litter far less tiring to carry. Nylon webbing, even bandanas tied together or strips of cloth or canvas can be used for shoulder straps. Carrying a litter in the hands—even if there are four bearers—causes hands to become very tired and cold. Frequent change-offs and exchanging sides are necessary. The frame of the sled shown here can easily be modified to adapt it to a hand-carried litter.

If your party is on skis, your impulse will probably be to construct a sled. Building a sled takes some time and equipment. If you merely tie a couple of cross pieces on the victim's skis, then attach the victim in his sleeping bag, you will end up, most likely, with a wet, cold victim who's worse off than he was when you started.

In using a sled, you have to be super-safe. The disabled person cannot care for himself; you have to do it for him. Special care may be necessary due to the nature of the injury. Also, the injured will not be active and thereby subject to cold more than the sled bearers.

The sled described here assumes that you have the equipment to build it. The original was made with the use of only an eight-inch saw, and a sharp knife a three-inch blade. Each joint was lashed with at least two loops of 550 cord (parachute line). The lashing was fastened as illustrated with two twists to the starting overhand knot and finished with a square knot with an extra twist in the first or overhand part of the knot. This type of square knot does not require a borrowed finger to keep the knot tight while finishing it. It also holds much more securely in nylon cord than a regular square knot.

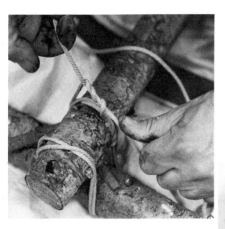

Tying the sled crosspieces—An extra twist in beginning the knot will provide extra security.

The lashing completed with a regular square knot.

Modify this sled if you feel so inclined. The design shown, however, takes into consideration the design elements of the cross-country ski. These are, namely, that the front part of the ski, the shovel, is very flexible and that the ski is constructed to have the weight carried at the middle where the binding is mounted. The sled allows the shovels freedom to flex with the weight being carried by the middle of the ski.

Materials. (see list titled "Tool Kit" at the end of this article.)

A saw—The usual kind is a pull saw, not a push saw. Pushing hard will cause this type of saw to bend and perhaps break. Rubbing a little paraffin on the sides will make the cutting job easier, particularly with wet wood.

Completed sled before the addition of padding.

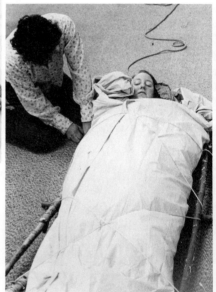

A demonstration showing the sled with passenger.

About 36 feet of nylon 550 cord—There are 16 joints that must be secured and three more that you may want to tie. Each joint takes about two feet of cord

At least four crosspieces about 30" long and 2-2½" in diameter—These will be the main foundation of your sled and should be carefully selected for strength. (Remember that is is illegal to cut living trees in many wilderness areas. Emergency may be taken into consideration by the authorities, but what is an emergency to you may not seem like one to them. Make every effort to construct the sled from downed wood. The materials must be strong in order to build a safe sled, however.

Notches in the crosspieces pro-   A clove hitch is used to attach
vide greater strength and stability.   the belay rope to all cross members.

Two diagonal pieces about 60" x 1-1½" in diameter–These should be a bit
more flexible than the crosspieces so they will flex with the weight of the rider.

Two side pieces about 6-7" long and 2" or so in diameter–These serve three
main functions: to push some of the snow away from the injured person, to serve
as handles for lifting the sled over obstacles and to act as "bumpers" to protect
the injured from objects such as trees and rocks. These pieces should be quite
straight and free from limb stubs that would reduce their effectiveness.

The skis–Use the heaviest skis in the group, not necessarily those belong-
ing to the injured person.

**The injured person is tied to the belay rope by a separate line to assure
his safety in the event that the sled pulls apart. One should learn how to
tie this knot (bowline on a coil) before going on the trip.**

Large waterproof tarp of at least 6' x 8'—If no tarp is available, you might consider using a tent or tent fly (although with the current cost of tents, you might want to give this some extra thought). If a polyethelene tarp is used, great care is required not to tear it. This is particularly difficult if the snow is icy.

Ensolite pads—Use all the pads in the group to place over the protuberences in the sled and to insulate the rider from the cold snow. Use extra clothing, parkas and anything else you can spare to provide additional insulation for the injured person.

Examine the illustration of the sled and note that the forward-most crosspiece is not fastened to the skis but only to the side pieces. This allows the shovels of the skis to flex, thus giving the injured person a more comfortable ride. The side pieces are also fastened on top of the remaining crosspieces. This permits the skis to be in contact with the snow while the side pieces tend to ride above

Notice, too, that the three crosspieces are securely lashed to the skis and that they are notched to fit the skis. This creates a very secure foundation upon which the rest of the sled can be built.

After you have constructed the sled according to the directions, you have to make it ready for the rider. Position the tarp so it extends evenly over the whole sled. Then pile on the ensolite pads and the rest of the padding. Now lie on the sled yourself to check it for comfort. It may need modifications. Use the extra clothing, insert more cross pieces and do whatever is necessary to improve the sled's comfort. Save the victim's pack for a back support or pillow.

When you're satisfied that no more improvements are needed, place the victim on the sled (the person should be in a sleeping bag, of course). If the weather is cold, you might want to place a couple of hot water canteens inside the sleeping bag as heat sources.

After the rider is placed on the sled, fold the tarp over him starting with the feet or head first (see next section) so the snow will not enter under the tarp and cause the injured to become wet and cold. The rider will usually object if you cover his face, so fold the tarp leaving his face uncovered. Now, using the remainder of your 550 cord, lace the injured to the sled. Make sure the lacing isn't too tight or too loose. If it's too tight then the insulating value of the sleeping bag may be lost or at least decreased; too loose and snow will enter.

HEAD FORWARD OR BACK?

The terrain will mainly determine whether the injured should be placed with his head to the front of the sled or the rear. If the terrain to the road head is mostly uphill, the rider will want his head at the ski-tip end of the sled. If it's downhill, he will probably want his head at the tail end. Of course, it's not too difficult to unlace the injured person from the sled and turn him around if the situation requires.

PULLING AND STEERING THE SLED

Ski poles were left out of the construction of the sled for this purpose. The poles are carefully fastened, two at the front, two at the rear, to the side pieces of the sled. The poles at the head of the sled are used mainly for pulling the sled and the ones at the rear are mainly for steering. (In crossing unknown terrain, you might scout out the best route before taking the sled through.) The poles must be securely attached. If they come loose, you could lose the whole sled.

   A much easier way to move the sled, particularly uphill and downhill, is by using the 100 feet of 9mm rope listed in "Optional Items" on page 84. Attach the rope to the front of the sled, tying a knot around the first crosspiece and the other crosspieces. Leave about six feet of rope extending behind the sled. This "tail" will be used to steer the sled.

   Using the rope, three people can move this sled almost anywhere. The techniques for the various types of terrain are as follows.

   Uphill Technique: One person stays with the sled to steer it and to attend to the injured. Two people ski out ahead to the very end of the rope or to a spot where they can get a good, stable foothold. Then, they begin to haul in the rope hand over hand with the help of the person attending the sled. When they have pulled the sled to a safe spot where it is in no danger of escaping, they secure the sled and repeat the procedure. It may be necessary to swing the sled sideways to the hill so it won't slide forward or backward while the rope is being carried ahead.

   If a larger party is available, four to six people, then the uphill progress can be almost continuous. A skier skis out with the rope as it is being retrieved by a second party that does the pulling.

   Remember that you do not have to go straight up the hill. You can traverse as many times as needed. A smaller group will probably make more traverses than a larger, stronger one.

   Technique on the flat: Each member of the party grabs a loop of rope and pulls. Again the sled is steered by the "tail" at the back.

   Downhill technique: If there are trees around and you have a nylon sling and a minimum of three carabiners (snap links), then the job of moving the sled downhill can be an easy one. If there are no trees, etc., you will have to make many traverses and use the utmost care in guiding the sled down the hill. The braking technique illustrated (page 82) should be carefully followed. Notice that the gates of the 'biners are always placed opposite each other. This way a 'biner cannot accidentally open and allow the rope to run free. The knot used to join the ends of the sling must be a secure one. There are several ways to accomplish this. A simple but effective way is with the familiar fisherman's knot.

   In this downhill technique the sled is essentially belayed down the hill. The belayer (the person standing behind the tree—now called the belay point) can stop even an out-of-control headlong descent by merely wrapping the end of the rope, which is going through the carabiner brake, a one-half turn around the tree. On gentle hills the sled may have to be pulled slightly to make it run. The belayer must never let the rope go once he has agreed to belay the sled down the hill. He must be constantly alert to the movement of the sled and take appropriate action to guide it safely down the hill. It's also important not to rush this procedure.

   Being super-safe is the only approach to take! When the belay rope is about 20 feet from the end, the belayer calls out "Twenty feet." This will alert those attending the sled to look for a new belay point and to secure the sled as necessary. I like to tie a large bulky knot at the very end of the rope when I'm belaying. Then if I'm overtaken by some unforeseen catastrophe, the sled will come to a definite, if sudden, stop.

   When in doubt about the steepness of a hill, belay! It's a speedy and safe way to descend. For practice, start on a small hill. This will educate you on what to expect when you get to a real steep hill.

On a steep hill you may want to attach or tie in the rider to the belay rope. This is most easily done with a separate shorter rope. Tie a bowline snugly around the injured person, then attach the shorter rope to the tail of the belay rope using an overhand figure-eight loop in the belay rope and a bowline in the short rope. Make certain that there is enough slack between the tie-in rope and the belay rope so that the rider is not pulled continually by the belay rope.

If you don't trust the strength of the cross pieces or if the skis have metal edges that may cut the 550 cord lashing, then the above prodecure is recommended. Metal-edged skis should also have the edges under the rope lashings covered with a couple of layers of adhesive tape.

WORTHWHILE HINTS

Remember that the injured person is likely to feel that he's being a big bother to everyone. You can do much to relieve this guilt feeling by including the victim in the decision-making process. Let the injured person know that it's a positive experience to evacuate someone, and that the evacuation process will usually be good for many evenings' worth of stories.

Don't try and emulate those ski patrol experts who can singlehandedly take a fully loaded sled down the steepest downhill with dexterity and abandon. It's foolhardy and potentially disastrous—unless you're an expert. Few skiers have the patrolman's training, equipment or experience. Also, regular cross-country skis don't have the steel edges and heel bindings to give you the control that the ski patrolman gets on his alpine skis. So play it safe!

Often fellow skiers you meet along the trail want to help. Some of them can be useful. Others are often merely curious and want to know what happened. In the latter case they can be more of a hindrance than a help.

Trail gossip often exaggerates the situation to an unbelievable degree. It might not be inappropriate to "white lie" a bit and tell the curious that you're only practicing an evacuation. But if you really need help, don't be afraid to ask. Many people who ski cross country are medical experts and can be of immense assistance. Who knows? The person you might run into on the trail might be a physician.

IN SUMMARY

If the injury is not serious, merely incapacitating, and no further injury is sustained by the victim, then the evacuation can be quite an adventure. But play it safe! Take all essential equipment with you. Have the utmost regard for your wilderness environment. If possible, cut only limbs for your sled and not whole trees. If you can, use only downed wood. If you need to cut down a whole small tree, try to select one that is crowded by other trees, and would stunt itself or another tree anyway.

Make certain the sled is sound; check the knots and lashings before any downhill run is attempted. Learn to tie a sound bowline, figure-eight knot and

Larry Moitozo demonstrates the technique of belaying a sled downhill utilizing a carabiner brake. To bring the sled to a secure stop the rope is merely wrapped a half-turn around the tree. (Inset) Carabiner brake.

fisherman's knot before you go into the woods. Square knots do not hold well in nylon rope.

A careful evacuation can be a positive personal experience; a careless one can be a tragedy.

TOOL KIT

Essential Items:

● Small pair of "water pump" type pliers—The type with adjustable jaws is much more versatile.

● Small pair of side cutters—If these are carefully resharpened they not only cut easier (even fish hooks) but need less pressure to cut. They are fragile but can cut heavy metal if used gently.

● 10-20' of iron wire—this is the modern version of baling wire. Two or three of the new flimsy coat hangers will do.

● 8 or so six-penny nails—Useful as nails, can be modified into rivets or clevis pins, etc.

● 50 or more feet of parachute cord (550 cord)—Useful for everything from shoe laces to head bands.

● 4" x 4" piece of paraffin—For starting fires, de-icing skis, freeing balky zippers.

● Strong but lightweight screwdriver—Wooden handles are lighter than plastic.

● Sharp multi-tooled knife—The authentic Swiss Army Officer's Knife is hard to beat.

● Full roll of 3" waterproof adhesive tape—in addition to one in your medical kit.

Optional Items:

● 100+ feet of nylon rope—Either the 9mm or 3/8" diameter.

● 30-40 feet of 1" nylon webbing.

● Minimum of three (preferably six) oval carabiners.

GROUND TO AIR SYMBOLS

In an emergency, it's often vitally important to be able to signal information to aircraft in the area. Below is the accepted code for ground-to-air signals. The symbols should be stamped out in the snow in 20-40 foot sizes.

LL	**I**	**II**	**X**	**K**	**↑**
All is well	Require M.D.	Require Medical Supplies	Unable to proceed	Indicate direction to proceed	Proceeding in direction of arrow
△	**F**	**N**	**Y**	**⌐L**	**□**
Safe to land here	Need Food and H_2O	No	Yes	Not understood	Need map & compass

5

Safe Winter Motoring

by Beverly Wilcox Robinson

Beverly Wilcox Robinson, musicologist, french horn player and guerilla automobile mechanic ("If you can drive it, you can fix it!"), grew up in New York State and spent the winter of '73 living in Rochester and commuting to her job in Syracuse, 90 miles away.

I left Rochester, N.Y., just before dark. Must be in Syracuse by eight. Poor visibility, 14 inches of new snow on the ground already, and the storm is showing no signs of letting up. On the radio I hear that the New York State Thruway was closed 20 minutes after I got on it. Have seen no other cars so far.

A dim glow in the rear view mirror catches my eye. A car is approaching— much too fast. The speedometer of my ancient but faithful Volkswagen registers 25 mph. I quickly—too quickly—duck out of the passing lane. The rear wheels, still patiently grinding forward, fishtail out to my left. I steer back towards the left—just the right amount—to stop the skid. Too much correction and I would have been spun around into the path of the approaching car. I accelerate slightly as the rear wheels pass directly behind the front ones and I am safe, just as the car, a Cadillac with Florida plates, flashes by at twice my speed. His slipstream carries a blinding cloud of powdery white snow.

Twenty minutes and six miles later, a truck overtakes me. His high beams blaze briefly to warn me. I answer (headlights off-on, off-on) and he passes. A quick flip of my high beams invites him to pull back in front of me.

I accelerate to match his speed and follow his cheerful red taillights all the way to Syracuse at a comfortable 34 mph. On the way, we pass the Florida Cadillac, resting in the large, flat field the highway engineers specifically designed for errant cars and their drivers. I make a note of the next mileage marker to report it to the attendant at the toll collection booth.

How does one learn winter driving? By practice. I grew up in New York State, and when I was old enough, my mother had me drive her to the store after a bad storm. Creeping along at 10 mph, I must have skidded into the snowbanks six or eight times, and each time we pushed the car back out of the drift left by the snowplow, two women against a huge old Ford. But I continued until I

learned the new rules of the game. Snow driving isn't much more risky or difficult than any other kind of driving. You just have to learn a few more of the law
of physics.

ACCELERATION

The first of these laws concerns acceleration. In physics, acceleration is de-
fined as a change in either speed or direction of motion, and your car can "accelerate," in this sense, in any of four directions—right, left, forward or backward. I
your car is already travelling forward and you do not accelerate in any of these
directions, the car will continue to travel straight forward, no matter how slippery the surface on which you are driving.

The first rule of winter driving is to change speed or direction as little as
possible. When you need to turn *right or left*, do it as slowly as possible. The pr
lem to avoid is having your front wheels start to make the turn while your rear
wheels continue forward, throwing the car sideways into a skid. This unhappy
state of affairs is almost guaranteed to happen if you apply your brakes during th
turn, by the way, so be sure to slow down before you get to the turn. With a little practice, you will be able to estimate quite accurately how fast you can take
the turn without skidding.

There will be times, however, when skidding cannot be avoided, when
the car begins to skid on its own due to irregularities in the road surface, wind,
ice patches or too-rapid acceleration. Think of it the way you thought of the
clutch when you were learning to drive a standard-shift car. At first using the
clutch was strange and frightening, but with a little practice it became just anoth
part of your repertoire.

To get out of a skid you must realign the car so that it is facing the direction in which it is travelling. (This is not necessarily the direction in which you want to travel: in the illustration on pages 88-89, the car is still travelling forward, even though the driver wanted to go to the left.) To recover, you must steer back towards the side the rear end is on, sort of like a dog chasing its tail. When your front wheels and back wheels are all going forward again, you can gently return to your desired path and have at it again, this time more slowly. Keep the car in gear. This produces better control and also slows the car down.

Keep in mind that it's possible to oversteer and have the back wheels sneak out from under you on the other side. This is especially a problem in rear-engine cars such as the Porsche, Corvair or Volkswagen, or front-engine cars carrying a lot of weight in the trunk. (Some drivers carry a couple hundred pounds of sand or concrete blocks in the trunk all winter to give them extra traction: the increase in traction is not noticeable, but the tendency to "wipe out" going around corners is.)

Anyway, to avoid this, you must straighten out the front wheels as the car comes back under control. This becomes automatic after the first or second try. If you misjudge it and start to straighten too late, simply steer towards the side to which the rear wheels have swung. Of course, you must *never* step on the brakes when the car is skidding. For reasons to be discussed later, braking is the one sure way to lose all control over the car's speed and direction.

Some sections of the road are more slippery than others. If you have to go over a bridge, or a shaded spot, or under an overpass, steer straight ahead and do not change speed. It helps to be on the lookout for these spots so you can slow down before you come to them.

Accelerating *forward* too quickly isn't nearly as serious a problem at high (over 20 mph) speeds, although it can still cause skidding. Actually, a small, steady increase in speed is a great help in keeping your car under control. But acceleration becomes a problem when you are in danger of getting stuck—on a steep, icy hill, for example. Here your problem is to keep the rear wheels from spinning. If you give the engine too much gas, the wheels will lose traction and spin, causing your car to grind slowly and with a loud howling sound to a halt. The trick here is to never come to a stop, because once you stop, you're stuck. When you hear or feel the wheels spinning, let up on the gas and the inertia of the car will carry you away from the slippery spot. Apply the gas gently and you can continue. On most cars, if one rear wheel spins, the car is just as stuck as if both were spinning.

This situation epitomizes the whole winter driving situation. On dry pavement, the whole American *macho* trip prevails—who spent the most money for his metal masculinity symbol? Who is the big man that can step the hardest on the accelerator pedal? In winter, the big man behind the wheel is the one who has learned the most about his equipment, has the most experience and can think clearly in a panic situation.

Negative acceleration, more commonly known as "deceleration," is accomplished either by braking, letting up on the gas to slow down, or both. This is perhaps the most difficult situation to learn to deal with in driving on snow. In times of panic, the instinct is to hit the brake—the harder the better.

Brakes work by applying friction simultaneously to the inside of each of the four wheels. When the friction between the wheel and the brake shoe is more than the friction between the wheel and the road, the wheel will instantly stop turning. If all four wheels stop turning, your car will be turned into a giant hockey puck, its line of travel and distance of travel before coming to rest determined solely by its inertia. If only some of the wheels stop turning (if your brakes are out of adjustment) the situation is even worse, since your car will spin in circles.

Thus, your brakes are absolutely useless in slippery conditions, and they are especially dangerous in situations where the car is already partially out of control. When you must use them (where there's a good chance you'll be able to stop), "fan" them—that is, apply them for a second, then let up to get the wheels started rolling again. Repeat this process as necessary until the car is stopped. Naturally, it takes a long time to stop on slippery roads: three to 12 times as long as on dry pavement, in fact. Travel well below the speed limit and allow extra distance between you and the car in front of you. This way you will not have to make any sudden—and dangerous—moves.

It's a good idea to try your brakes lightly once to twice when you first start out, just to get the feel of how slippery the road is.

Finally, be sure to wear your seatbelt. If you spin off the road, it can make the difference between a harmless scare and a tragic accident.

PRACTICE

Everybody makes a few mistakes when learning something new. Make sure that your learning situation is not one where your mistakes might kill you. Some eastern cities hold ice-driving clinics on frozen lakes. These are lots of fun and teach you more than reading 10 articles about winter driving. For practicing on your own, deserted parking lots are dandy. Try to work in some practice of winter driving skills before you need to use them to get where you're going.

VISIBILITY

The other great problem in winter driving is visibility. In winter there is an increased probability of some inexperienced or overconfident driver hitting you. To drive defensively, you must be able to see in all directions. Here are some assorted facts about visibility:

● *Headlights:* Use low beams in snow or fog. High beams reflect off whatever is suspended in the air and blind you. When visibility is poor, turn on your lights to make your car more visible to other drivers. Remember to clean the dirt/ice/snow/road salt off the headlights every time you stop. Also, knock off those pieces of ice that form behind the wheels. They can limit your steering se-

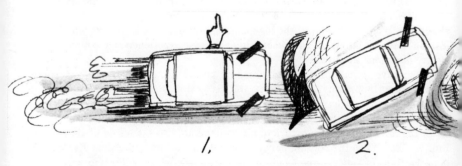

1.   *2.*

verely when they get too big, and occasionally they freeze to the tires when left overnight.

● *Windshield Wipers/Cleaner:* Department stores sell special formulas to put in your windshield cleaner tank. These formulas will not freeze in cold weather and will cut through all the stuff that collects on your windshield. Road salt, which forms nice crystal patterns all over the windshield, is impervious to anything but commercial windshield cleaner. In a pinch, rubbing alcohol will do, but if it stands overnight it settles out of the water and the water then freezes. Be sure your windshield wiper blades are in good condition.

● *Windshield Scraper:* While your car is warming up in the morning, scrape ice and snow off all windows with a plastic (not metal) scraper. If you don't have one (they're hard to come by in parts of the country where it doesn't snow), a pancake turner (plastic), a credit card or the top of a pocket comb will do.

● *Fog:* Perhaps the most difficult problem is defrosting the insides of your windows after you get the car started. There are two reasons why your windows fog up. The first is the difference in temperature between the inside and outside of the car. A cold window will collect "dew" just as a cold iced tea glass does in summer. The second reason is the humidity generated by several people in warm coats sitting, and breathing, inside a warm car with all the windows rolled up.

There are a number of things you can do to keep the insides of your windows clear. Unfortunately, none of them are entirely satisfactory. You can (1) keep wiping the fog away with a cloth. This has the advantage of giving immediate results, but must be repeated every 10 seconds or so. You can also (2) turn on the defroster, which is usually a contraption that blows hot air on the front window only, forcing the fog to evaporate and condense even more heavily on the un-defrosted wondows. Perhaps the best solution is to (3) open all the windows, which gets rid of both the excess humidity and the difference in temperature. This is also good for keeping the driver from getting sleepy.

For those (including me) who object to such Spartan methods as the last one, a combination of all three is the best solution. Turn on the heat or defroster, open the windows a little, and wipe up any stubborn patches with a cloth. I have also heard that the air conditioner will take care of fog through its dehumidifying effect, but anyone who would rather turn on the air conditioning than roll down the window probably isn't interested in outdoor winter recreation anyway, right?

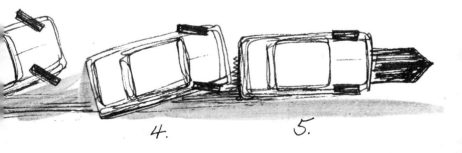

4.   5.

GETTING THE CAR IN MOTION

Probably the next most frustrating problem for the winter motorist is getting the car in motion when it has been parked on snow. The story is all too familiar: You brush the snow off your car, warm up the engine, step on the gas, and all that happens is the howl of the two rear wheels spinning. What now?

First of all, don't spin the wheels. As you may already have noticed, that just digs them in deeper. Some people recommend starting the car in second gear if the car is a standard shift. Using the second gear gives the car less power than first gear and less power should mean less chance of spinning. I prefer to use first gear and to go easy on the gas.

Make sure your front wheels are pointed straight ahead. If they are turned to one side, it will be considerably more difficult for the rear wheels to push them forward through the snow. If the snow is deep, shovel out a pathway in front of the front wheels for 10 feet or so to decrease the rolling resistance even further and give the car a "running start."

If this doesn't work, you can try "rocking" out. Move the car forward and backward alternately, synchronizing your accelerations with the natural movement of the car towards the deepest part of the rut. This is fairly easy in an automatic, but something of a feat in a clutch car.

If this doesn't work, you have to get out and start trying more drastic measures. Try having all your passengers sit on the trunk of the car to put more weight over the rear wheels. More weight above the rear wheels is dangerous when moving, but it can help you get unstuck when you're standing still.

The next step is having your passengers push the car. Be careful not to let the wheels spin, as snow and ice and other unpleasant objects will fly up from the wheels and hit those who are pushing. Again, be sure your front wheels are pointed straight ahead. As a last resort, you can shovel dirt, sand or rocks under the rear wheels to give them traction. This assumes that you brought a shovel *and* some sand—four or five pounds of it.

If you are trying to get up an icy hill, you should back down and get a running start. Obviously, it is also a good idea to park facing downhill or out of your parking space, as the above techniques are much simpler in forward than reverse.

THE BETTER PART OF VALOR

A little foresight will keep you out of most of the above situations. Try to avoid driving in blizzards, when the temperature is hovering right at the freezing point (the roads are the most slippery then) or at night. Also try to stay off isolated roads where no one will find you if you get stuck. Mountain roads are also to be avoided, since the consequences of sliding off a corner in the road can be disastrous. This may all sound pretty obvious, but one look at the Friday night traffic on a mountain road to a popular ski resort when it's 34 degrees and snowing like the dickens is proof that it still needs to be said.

CAR CAMPING IN THE SNOW

I have a stubborn natural aversion to paying someone a lot of money for a place to sleep. After all, I'm not even going to be conscious to appreciate what I'm paying all that money for. Because of these odd views, I have slept in my car (or beside it) in nearly every state of the union.

There is a special technique in doing this in the winter, however. A car is

one of the worst devices for conserving warmth yet invented. All those windows and large areas of thin metal (like the roof) conspire to get rid of heat as quickly as possible. About all your car is good for is shelter from the wind. My old Volkswagen had rust holes in it from the road salt and wasn't even good for that.

Nevertheless, once in a while there comes a time when camping in your car in the snow is desirable, either for financial reasons or because you've managed to get it stuck somewhere overnight.

Do not depend on your car heater to keep you warm. If you do, you run the risk of carbon monoxide poisoning.

Carbon monoxide, a by-product of your car's internal combustion process, is odorless, colorless and tasteless. It tends to rise upward. Since you're probably sitting right above your car's exhaust system when you're at the wheel, unless you have a rear-engine car, you can imagine the possibilities. Worse still, the first sign of carbon monoxide poisoning is a feeling of drowsiness, so you don't realize what's happening to you.

Suppose you are stuck overnight—say, you were driving up to the mountains to ski on a Friday night after work, you missed a sharp corner and landed in a snowy field, unhurt, but unable to climb the three-foot embankment up to the road. It's one o'clock in the morning and you have seen no cars passing in the hour you have already been there. You decide to wait until morning and then flag down a ride to the nearest town. So far so good.

You start to get cold, and you're tired from driving. So you figure you'll run the engine for five minutes to warm the car up enough so you'll be able to get some sleep. Later when the car gets too cold again, you'll wake up and run the engine for a few more minutes.

This works well the first time. You warm the car, turn off the engine and go to sleep. You wake up in an hour and warm up the car again. When you wake up a second time—it's now 4:30 in the morning—you warm up the car, but the combination of all that nice heat and your drowsiness allows you to go to sleep with the engine still running. Too bad.

It helps to be prepared if there's any possibility you could get stuck overnight in the snow. Make it a habit of throwing your down sleeping bag or a bunch of blankets (or both) in the trunk. At least you'll have the blankets to lie on while you're struggling to install the snow chains. If you need to use the blankets for an overnight stay, drape some of them over the seats to make a "tent." This will provide considerably better heat conservation. Sleep with a window open a crack to let in fresh air. Run the engine perhaps once to get the car warm enough so you can go to sleep. If it's severely cold, you'd better start thinking of ways to stay awake until dawn so you don't freeze to death in your sleep. Exercise serves the dual purpose of keeping you warm and awake, but avoid getting so much exercise that you perspire heavily and hypothermia becomes a problem.

If you leave your car, even for a short time, leave your turn signals flashing. This will indicate that you have been in the area recently and are planning on returning soon. If you use the radio or lights, be careful not to drain the battery so much that you can't start the car. You can run gadgets with the engine on and the generator/alternator will provide the power and leave your battery charge intact. Again, beware of falling asleep. Your supply of gas will last a lot longer if you do not race or rev the engine.

If you have company, two people can stay warmer than one—but, of course, you already know that. All the advice about staying warm to be found elsewhere in this book applies here. Just remember that even though you paid a lot of money for your car, it will not keep you warm. But you can keep yourself warm with a certain amount of ingenuity and foresight. With this thought in mind, consider the list at the end of this chapter showing items to bring along when driving in snow.

GETTING OUT

A word of caution: stay with your car! You are at least near a road, and sooner or later somebody will come by and help you. If you walk for help, you can get lost or cold or tired, and you won't have the shelter your car can provide. Trust the highway patrol and/or snowplow to come along sooner or later. The highway patrol and the snowplow crews know that motorists get stranded when it snows, and they're on the lookout. Remember that many motorists have died trying to walk out when they would have lived had they stayed with their car.

Another thing to remember is that you can go 30 days or more without food—and it will probably do you more good than harm (at least that's what authorities on fasting such as Herbert Shelton, Are Waerland and Dick Gregory say). The first few days you feel hungry, but then the hunger goes away, and if you're not worried by all the stories you heard as a child about people starving to death in a week, you'll feel fine (in fact, better than usual) for another two weeks or so. When you start to feel hungry again, starvation has begun.

When you get thirsty, melt some snow into water. If you eat snow, you will get chills, and it won't satisfy your thirst anyway. It takes about 10 cups of snow to make one cup of water. For a heat source to melt the snow you can use either the sun or the heat from your car's engine.

CHAINS AND SNOW TIRES

Snow tires have a special tread pattern that gets more of a grip on the road than normal tires. Usually they have big rubber "teeth" around the edges, and sometimes they can be equipped with studs, which are nail-like objects that stick down into the road surface. Studs make driving on snow and ice a lot easier, but they are illegal in some states, or during certain times of the year in others, because they chew up the pavement. On dry pavement they also chew up your tires.

Snow tires are a lot less bother than chains because you put them on your

car and forget about them until spring. They can be used on dry pavement with no special problems. It is not legal to substitute them for chains in some western states that have chain control, but their use is almost universal in the eastern US and Canada. (In the east, chain control is not necessary because all the drivers who refuse to use snow tires or chains are no longer on the road by the second week of winter!)

Snow tires can be mounted on the rear wheels only or on all four wheels. Your cornering ability is improved about 25% when you use snow tires on all four wheels, but you can get by on two. Snow tires should be mounted on their own rims so that they can be installed quickly and easily at home, or when you need them on the road.

Chains are a pain in the _ _ _ to install. Drivers who can put up with installing them, however, swear that there is no better way to give a car traction in the winter. They have the advantage of being small and easily portable, but they cannot be used at high speeds and they cannot run on dry pavement for long, so they must be removed and installed frequently during the winter. If you only drive in snow six or seven times a winter to go skiing, chains are probably your best choice.

There are two schools of chain installing. The first is the "back over" school. You park your car out of the way (not beside a highway), lay the chains out behind the wheels, and back the car up until the tires are on top of the chains. You then fasten the chains and drive away—supposedly. There are a few other things to remember:

(1) It is difficult, but necessary, to get the chains as tight as possible. Loose chains will wear out quickly, and they tend to chew up the tires. It is even more difficult to get the chains tight when your fingers are freezing and you're sitting in the middle of a snow drift, so remember to put them on early.

(2) Make sure you know how the fasteners work. Some of them are like those patented can openers that no one but the guy who invented it can figure out.

(3) Fasten the inner chain first. You won't be able to see what you're doing, and you'll be sitting there in the snow embracing with tender affection an ugly old automobile tire, so don't make things even more difficult by tightening the outside chain first.

(4) Buy tensioners for your chains. They are springs that take up some of the slack on the chains, and they pay for themselves in added tire and chain life. Be sure to put them on the inside of the wheel as well as the outside. If you've ever heard the sound of a chain breaking, you'll know why I recommend them.

(5) Stop after a mile or two and tighten the chains another link. As they heat up they get bigger, and what was a snug fit becomes loose and sloppy.

(6) When all else fails, *read the directions!*

It is a little easier to do all of these things if you belong to the second school of chain installing, the "jack up" school. You jack up one wheel at a time and install the chain. This procedure is easier in many ways, but it can be dangerous to jack up a car that's standing on ice and snow. Block all the wheels, pack snow behind the blocks, and dig through to the ground for a solid base on which to rest the jack. In addition, always work in such a manner that if the car fell, you wouldn't be caught underneath. When you finally get the chains on, remember to drive slowly—30 mph is a good speed, and 50 is really pushing it.

PREPARING YOUR CAR FOR WINTER

Have the engine tuned up to minimize the trouble of starting in cold weather. The brakes should be adjusted so that all four wheels will brake evenly. Put anti-freeze in the radiator so that it won't freeze and crack the engine block. Put in whatever grade of oil your local expert recommends, although the fact is no one in the world really knows what kind of oil you should use in your car.

A good safe choice is 10W-40 oil. They say it has a high viscosity even when it's hot, so it can still lubricate your engine, and a low viscosity when it's cold, so your engine can turn over and start in the morning. Since I have a Volkswagen (four of them, in fact) and the engine is cooled by the oil (instead of water), I'm a little afraid this wonderful liquid will forget itself and have a low viscosity when the engine is hot, thus raising the engine temperature above its normal 350°, so I use monograde oil. When I'm going around town in the winter, or making a trip of less than three hours, I use straight 10 weight. If I'm going to be on the road a long time I up it to 20 weight, but then I have trouble starting when it's cold.

By the way, STP and other oil treatments work by thickening your oil, so you don't need them in the winter. In fact, you can't use them.

Finally, get your battery in the very best condition possible. Buying a new one isn't a bad idea. Fill it with distilled water and clean the terminals so that they're making good contact. In cold weather the battery not only has to turn the engine over a lot longer than usual to start it, but the oil is going to be thick as molasses, which will make it harder than usual to turn the engine.

STARTING THE ENGINE

This is the classic problem of winter driving, and there are almost as many theories of how to start a car in cold weather as there are winter drivers. For those unfamiliar with the problem, consider the following:

In the mid-1920s, Ferdinand Porsche designed and tested a series of small cars that eventually culminated in the Volkswagen. The Daimler-Benz Company stopped production on one of his models, claiming the car would not start in cold weather.

Fifteen of the cars were parked overnight in the company lot and Porsche was challenged to start even one of them. He failed. After a bitter argument, he "flew into a rage, tore off his hat, trampled it in the snow, and marched out of the plant, never to return."

Here are a few principles to keep you out of similar situations:

● Be prepared by having a tuned-up engine with low viscosity oil in it, and have the spark plugs gapped a little closer than normal to make starting easier. Make sure your battery is in good condition. Batteries lose some of their voltage at cold temperatures, and a battery that is adequate in warm weather might not be in cold weather.

● Before you turn the ignition on, step on the gas once or twice. This extra gas will often be ignited by the first sparks when you turn the key to "start."

● Do not pump the gas while the engine is running. Just slowly floor the gas pedal while the engine turns and leave it there. If you pump the gas pedal, excess gas will flood the engine, and you will have to wait 10 minutes for it to evaporate before you can try to start the engine again. If your engine turns but will not start, and there is the odor of gas in the air, suspect that this has happened.

● If you are at high altitude and your car is not used to the thin air, open up the butterfly valve in the carburetor a bit. Here's how to find it: remove the air cleaner (that big round container-like object); you are now looking straight down the throat of the carburetor. You will see a round flap that should be covering the throat of the carburetor like a lid. This is the butterfly valve. Hold it open about a quarter of the way while someone else tries to start the car.

● If the car does not start in 15 seconds or so (especially if it doesn't even "cough"), stop and rest the battery for 10 or 20 seconds before you try again. On long try will drain the battery very quickly and soon your engine will be turning too slowly to start.

● If this happens, leave the car for an hour or so. Some of the charge will build up in the battery again.

● If all else fails, you can usually "pop start" a standard shift car. Turn the key to "on" (not "start"), put it in second gear, push the clutch pedal down, and have several people push the car—preferably downhill. When the car is going as fast as possible, yell "Banzai," "Dieu et mon droite!" "Allons!" or something equally appropriate, let out the clutch pedal, pump the gas for all you're worth, and pray a lot. Don't give up until the car has come to a dead stop, and dc let your pushers give up either. If the engine does start, don't "kill" it, or you'll have to do the whole thing over again, and probably you'll be a pusher this time.

● When you do get the car started, or even if it started easily, warm it up. A piece of metal at 30° is a different size than at 250°. Therefore, your engine is in very bad shape, so to speak, when it is cold. Also, a good warmup will decrease the danger of stalling in some inopportune place such as an intersection.

● If your car stalls persistently, you can raise the idling speed in the following manner: have a friend step on the gas pedal a couple of times while you look under the hood and see what moves. It should be a lever arm with a screw sticking out of the end. Give this screw a turn or so (clockwise) and see what that does. If it raises the idling speed somewhat but not too much, you have achieved the desired effect.

● This can be a bit anticlimactic: sometimes you finally get the engine started and then find the parking brake cable has frozen so the car won't move. When you park in a cold area, leave the parking brake off and keep your car rooted to the desired spot by leaving it in gear.

THINGS TO BRING ALONG

- snow shovel
- tow chain or rope
- snow tires or chains, plus tensioners, repair links and pliers.
- sand (4-5 lbs.)—be sure it is dry or it will freeze into a solid mass.
- blankets and/or down sleeping bag
- a can of Coke (to keep you awake—put it in the trunk to keep it cold)
- an ice scraper for the windshield
- boots & gloves
- paper towels and cloths to clean windshield and headlights
- extra can of windshield cleaner solution
- flashlight
- jack and wheel blocks
- this book.